THE POSTER

Its History and Its Art

DON QUIXOTE

FOR ERVINE WITH MY APPRECIATION
AND FRIENDSHIP— E. McKNIGHT KAUFFER

THE POSTER

Its History and Its Art

ERVINE METZL

WATSON-GUPTILL PUBLICATIONS

ACKNOWLEDGMENTS

No one produces a book like this without help. Many hearts and hands have gone into its making. Others whose names I list have done much more to make this book possible than can be adequately credited. They all have my everlasting gratitude.

Artists and friends who have lent me their posters were William A. Smith, Ella George, and, above all, Norman Kent, who helped editorially and contributed posters from his private collection. I am also indebted to Outdoor Advertising, Inc., The New York Public Library, The Croton Free Library, The Yugoslav Travel Information Bureau, The British Information Bureau, The London Underground and THE NEW YORK TIMES. Tony Venti Studios assisted with photographs of the posters. I must also acknowledge my debt to The Rev. Dan B. Brummitt, Ludwig Hohlwein, E. McKnight Kauffer, Fred G. Cooper and Ernst Lehner.

Finally, I must express my fervent thanks to Walter F. Kohn for his invaluable contributions, to Fairfax M. Cone for his comprehensive introduction, and to my wife, Isabella, for her execution of the book jacket.

CONTENTS

LIST OF COLOR PLATES

INTRODUCTION

ONE OF THE THINGS that will appear clear in the following lucid pages is the fact that appreciation of the poster both as an art form and as an advertising medium is continuously at ebb and flow. Why this should be it is possible to suggest by an analogy from the advertising business itself.

"First," it is said, "the artist becomes tired of the continuing treatment in a series of advertisements. Then the advertiser discovers that he, too, is bored with it. And so the idea is discarded — just about the time the public becomes aware of it." Later, usually, someone returns to it.

In this case, I can only hope that the long history of the poster that Ervine Metzl has put down with just the right emphasis on the truly important facts will, as he suggests, be repeated; but repeated over a much shorter space of years. By this I do not mean to project either the possibility or the desirability of a complete duplication of poster history (God forbid!), but only of some of its high lights.

For instance, I can't think of anything that would be a better substitute for the neon jungles of our city sidewalks than a retreat to the quiet and the beauty of some modern (but not too modern) adaptations of the oldest posters known, and the oldest advertising known: namely, the signs in Pompeii and the Herculaneum that were the precursors of the signs by which craftsmen and merchants attracted their custom throughout Europe during the Renaissance. Actually, of course, the locksmith's big key, the shoemaker's boot, and the jeweler's watch (with the hands painted always at twenty minutes after eight) were to be seen as long after the Renaissance as my own boyhood. For it is necessary to point out that we no longer have locksmiths and shoemakers and jewelers in the sense of even forty years ago. The locksmith now is in the back of a hardware store (except for one I saw recently in a shoe shining parlor which, itself, was in a garage which was in the basement of a tall office building). The shoemaker is no longer a shoe maker, but a vendor of the products of someone else's manufacture; the jeweler, except for some few very tony dealers, operates a bazaar where such un-jeweled objects as electric shavers and toasters, and cameras and ladies bags and pocketbooks are quite as important as clocks and watches and diamonds. The thing is, these varied wares are not easily symbolized. And a poster is above everything else a symbol.

Still, the brewer's signs that so gayly mark the pubs and the inns of England indicate what we *could* do in these and in some other lines. One of the things that a great many uneasy advertisers forget is that one more huge neon or electric sign only complicates the commercial scene. Four neon beer signs in the twin windows of a bar may make each of the brewers happy to see that they are there *too*, but a single neon sign, or better still, a well-designed and reasonably imaginative non-neon sign would surely be preferable from any sensible or sensitive standpoint. Nor am I speaking here only of aesthetic considerations. A man who decorates a bar or any other kind of retail establishment, or a highway, with a proliferation of signs (posters) is only proclaiming his lack of judgment and his lack of taste.

As you look carefully in Mr. Metzl's pages you will discover that over-signing has had its consequences before. While the prohibition against posters in France in the 16th century may have been dictated by their political and subversive aspects, it was surely imposed too, because of their great number. Conversely, indiscriminate and unregulated bill posting in England during the 19th century resulted in public protests that reached also into the vulgarity of what the author calls the pseudo-poster art.

Over-signing, then, is only one of the dangers that lurks in the path of poster redevelopment. Poor design is another. For it is an unhappy fact that a long series of these tends, not so much to challenge the artist to do better as to discourage the advertiser who must give him his opportunity. It is another unpleasant fact of life that we are today in the midst of just such a trend in America. The poster art which flourished in the 1890's and the 1920's, on magazine covers and on billboards, and which was an imaginative, deftly impressionistic art, has run head-on into the unimagination and (in the sense that it is all too perfect) the peculiar unreality of the still color photograph, and the moving picture of the television screen. It has run into them and crumpled at the impact. As a result, it may never be the same. The subtle hint of quality in a product and the promise that is made largely by the distinction of its making, are lost in the detailed, competitive argument that television makes possible and even ugly photographs endow with documentary authority. Furthermore, as Ervine Metzl says, the poster on the wall of the corner grocery store is gone along with the store itself (except in some very old neighborhoods), and highway posters seem no less likely to survive. Perhaps the latter shouldn't, either.

Advertising is something anyone can do and most people do badly. One result is the hideous signs that line so many of our older highways. Most of these, to be sure, are the business notices of small local retailers, gasoline filling stations, eating places and hotels. But their unsightliness has put a stigma on the outdoor poster generally, and posters are now banned insofar as this is possible on all of this country's new turnpikes and toll roads, and freeways. That this curtailment of circulation will make outdoor advertising less attractive competitively can hardly be doubted. When it is combined with growing disapproval, it may well be the end of such advertising as a major medium.

Nevertheless, I believe the future can be bright for poster art. It is important to remember that the poster was not always made in 24-sheets or 3-sheets, or even 1-sheet. Indeed, even today, many European posters are smaller. And I would guess that our most artistic and most effective posters in the near future will be very much smaller.

It may be that any hope for the replacing of a great many ugly, flashing neon and electric signs over the doors and in the windows of business houses, bars, gasoline stations and the like with artistic signs and honest, thoughtfully conceived and skillfully executed posters would be too sanguine. (This is written in Carmel, California, where neither neon nor electric signs are permitted; and the simply decorated unlighted wooden signs and the travel posters used as decorations are a delight.)

On the other hand, package and label design done upon the principles of the best poster design seems to offer endless, varied opportunity for a new generation of artists. It is only recently that, the values in artistic packaging have begun to emerge; and it is still more recently that the rules that apply to good posters have been discovered to be identical with those that pertain to good packages. Prior to these discoveries most American packages were complicated with wholly unnecessary detail. They were starkly and, often, frightfully literal. They made little or no concession to the possibility that the viewer might just be induced to identify himself (or herself) in some wholly desirable way with the product, thus greatly enhancing the product's promise. In other words, these packages took no advantage at all of the possibilities that lie in any communication when this is made in imaginative and emotional terms.

Just now there is great interest in packaging on the part of all industry. Artistic design has become a fetish with many a manufacturer. But too often he is badly prepared to cope with it. He forgets that no poster is really satisfactory unless it is clear what it is saying, that what is clear is also important, and that the identification of the viewer of the poster-package with the contents within must be demanding of action. On any other basis, the use of the package or the label as a poster is a matter of failure; and one for which there is no excuse.

The rules, as Mr. Metzl points out, are perfectly clear. However, they must be followed without exception. Break one rule and the jig is up. The poster is a failure; the package is a calamity.

Incidentally, one of the sorriest continuing exhibitions of the poster art in America today is made up of the parade of bad drawings and impossible ideas that decorate the U. S. postage stamp. The temptation to make many of these in the illustrative tradition of Currier and Ives prints has been too much for a literal-minded Post Office Department to withstand. Most of these stamps appear to have been contrived out of nothing good for a committee without taste or any notion at all of what makes a postage stamp dress up a letter. That it is the very same thing that makes a handsome poster dress up a wall as it delivers its message clearly and with the necessary impact seems not to have occurred to the postal authorities. I have hopes, just the same.

Just as I had come to believe that there was no current production of first-rate posters in our country, I was recently confronted with a magnificent example of the art in a single-sheet lithographed impression of San Francisco's waterfront, below Telegraph Hill, within the Golden Gate. Anything more than the name *San Francisco* in type would have been superfluous, and there was nothing more. Here was a poster that met the conditions this book sets out. The artist was the always exciting Dong Kingman.

With his example and all those that Ervine Metzl has so carefully and critically gathered here, my hope is that some talented people will turn to the poster with renewed interest and dedication. Out of their success can come a revitalized medium and a new national enjoyment.

December 1962
Carmel, California   *Fairfax M. Cone*

THE POSTER

Its History and Its Art

1

WHY THIS BOOK?

No one recognizes better than I that in presuming to write this book I am putting myself out on a limb. "What? Another poster book?" you may say. "Why?"

Why is precisely the reason for this book. Granted you have had posters paraded before your eyes for years in one annual after another, to say nothing of other books of posters that were compendia of certain schools or personal prejudices. I have my prejudices, too, and some of them will appear in subsequent pages. But this book has reasons for existence quite outside my prejudices; and the quickest way to justify and understand them is to review existing poster books.

The annuals need not concern us. They are necessary compilations created as source books for artists. Research workers of the future will find them valuable reflections of the prevalent taste of the year in which each of them was created, but they make no attempt whatever to consider the field historically.

This book, on the other hand, tries to see the poster in historical perspective, as a continuous evolution. I have found only two books that have done this before. Since both of them were written about fifty years ago,* they necessarily omit all mention of the tremendous changes posters have undergone since their day. They were excellent for their time, but although they viewed posters both historically and critically, they did not attempt to set poster development into the larger framework of the social, economic, and political considerations that had influenced it so profoundly. These considerations include *fin de siècle* decadence; the pall of Victorianism; the shaping of modern advertising in the United States, especially in the 1920's; the artistic doldrums of the two world wars; industrialization; the automobile; mass marketing; mass affluence; mass literacy, education, and sophistication; changes in taste, morals, and the mechanics of distribution; rampant nationalism; modern art; photography; and many others.

I am sure my readers will agree that these are all too important to be ignored. I hope to show how they all influenced and even determined the course of modern poster history. And, incidentally, how completely posters mirror their times.

Other poster collections striving for immortality between hard covers have in many cases confined themselves to showing the work of a single artist or a single school or trend. This means that their point of departure is in all cases that of the artist.

As an artist, I can only commend this but as a working creator of posters, I find it inadequate. Inadequate because too often it ignores or sidesteps the very purpose for which a poster is created: *to sell something.*

All you have to do is to look critically at the next ten posters you see to realize that some may be good advertising but poor art; or good art but poor advertising; or unsatisfactory both as art and as advertising.

Out on the limb I have chosen in these pages I insist that a good poster must be both good art *and* good advertising.

To understand this, I shall try to be specific, and determine what a poster is, what is does, how it does it, and what makes it succeed or fail.

A poster is a message dramatically expressed in terms of the graphic arts. Ideally, it should be so startling as to force its attention on every passer-by, so direct that it conveys its complete message in a flash, so simple that its meaning is unmistakable, so convincing that it is remembered long after it is out of sight.

Every new poster makes news — as surely as today's newspaper, and it *sells* its news. First to last, a poster *sells.*

Simpler, more direct, and more concentrated than any other kind of advertising, a poster goes straight to the point, says what it has to say, and stops there. It talks faster than you can, eliminates non-essentials, and, like a poem, vibrates with overtones and with its power of persuasion.

To do this, a poster must startle you — seize you by the eyes and hold you just long enough to register its message. That's all that's necessary. Like a sky-rocket, it has done its job: you'll remember it long after you've left it behind.

Look at the flag of Japan, the most perfect poster ever created. Located east of its nearest neighbors, Japan has always called herself "the Land of the Rising Sun." Her flag, a red sun rising in a white background, expresses this concept perfectly. It tells her story without a single word.

Just as effective, but at the opposite extreme, were the Packard automobile posters of the 1920's. They had no illustration at all, only the six simple words: *Ask the Man Who Owns One.*

Most posters, of course, use both words and pictures. Lucian Bernhard combined them perfectly in his poster for Priester Matches. Nothing more than two matches and the brand name.

Posters have been used to inform, exhort, and persuade, almost since language was reduced to writing. But the widespread commercial use of posters, and the development of poster art as a specialized technique, dates only from the 1880's.

In preparing this book, I have selected several hundred posters to illustrate the development of poster design through the years and the ways in which that development was affected by national and local habits and preferences, by the march of civilization, by the needs of the times, and by the genius of outstanding poster artists throughout the world.

Literally millions of posters have been designed and produced since the 1880's. Those I have selected for this study may represent neither the best nor the worst produced by their time or their creators. Limitations of space restricted my choice and in some cases it was no longer possible to get perfect copies of old posters I would like to have used. Copyright restrictions narrowed the selection still further.

But within these limitations, I do think the posters I have chosen are the most representative of the various trends that have made the modern poster what it is today. And like all good posters, they speak eloquently themselves.

*Walter von zur Westen: Reklamekunst, Bielefeld und Leipzig, 1914, Velhagen & Klasing; and Charles Matlack Price: *Poster Design,* New York, George W. Bricka, 1913; New and Enlarged Edition, 1922.

Poster for an English equilibrist and broad jumper, Nürnberg, 18th century

French theatre poster,
Paris, 1768

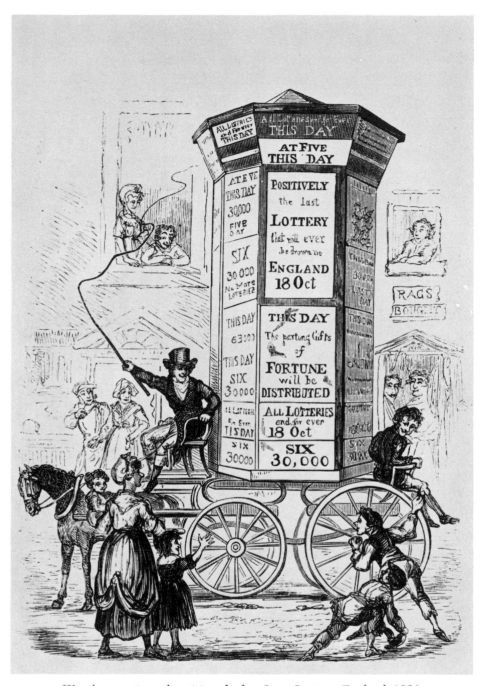

Wood engraving advertising the last State Lottery, England, 1826

Een schoene ghenuechlicke eñ seer vreede hystorie van eenre vrouwē gheheeten Meluzyne/ eñ van harer afcoemste eñ gheslachte vā haer voert ghecomen synde. eñ van harer alre wonderlike eñ vrome werckē eñ feyten die sy gedaē eñ bedieuen hebben Ende es nu nyewelyc we den wallsche ghetranslateert in duptsche / ende met schoonē personagen ende figueren na den epsch der materien verciert Ende mē salse met vele meer andere niewe boecken vinden te coopen ter plaetzen hier onder gheschieuen

The oldest known illustrated publisher's poster, printed in 1491 by
Gerhard Leeu, Antwerp, advertising his publication, an illustrated
book of the beautiful mermaid, Melusina

Portrait poster of the quack, Georg Faber, advertising his medicine
balls, for itch, mange, dandruff, blemishes, and for washing oil and
fat spots from garments. Designed by Jonas Umbach, Augsburg, 1648

*A wood engraving illustrating indiscriminate
bill posting in mid-19th century London*

2

POSTERS ARE NOT
EXACTLY NEW

NOBODY KNOWS WHO MADE THE FIRST POSTER. The Bible tells us that Moses
came down from Mount Sinai with a pair of tablets inscribed with the Ten
Commandments. The governments of antiquity published their laws on large
stone and bronze plaques and placed them, as we do our posters, in conspicuous
places.

Roman praetors and aediles used *alba*—wooden slabs painted white—on
which to inscribe their rules of office. These, too, were posted at what we would
call high traffic locations.

The excavations at Pompeii and Herculaneum have disclosed hundreds of
commercial posters. Many were electioneering posters, while others advertised
such familiar attractions as shows, inns, places for rent and articles lost or stolen
(with rewards for their return). Some were painted in black on the outside of
buildings, others were in red. They were particularly numerous on the walls of
the many bathhouses that were social centers in the Roman world.

Especially interesting is the facade of a Pompeiian building which is divided
into many white poster spaces whose arrangement suggests that they were probably sold or rented to advertisers, much as billboards are today. A good many of
them were done by an artist who was so proud of his work that he signed a
poster announcing a gladiatorial combat: *Scr. Aemilius Celer singulus ad lunam*
—"inscribed solely by Aemilius Celer, by moonlight." Celer not only signed his
work, he also advertised himself. *Aemilius Celer hic habitat*—"Aemilius Celer

lives here," reads another poster found among his sketches at Insula IX., 8, apparently Aemilius Celer's home and workshop.

Another Pompeiian poster announces that an inn calling itself "At the Sign of the Elephant" is now under the new management of a man named Sittius. A picture of an elephant is shown as the trademark.

From the excavations at Pompeii and Herculaneum alone, archaeologists have uncovered more than 1600 electioneering posters, advertising more than 100 candidates. This is apart from commercial posters. If a provincial town like Pompeii left us so many hundreds of posters, we can well imagine how many thousands more must have decorated the streets of such larger cities as Rome, Carthage, Ephesus, and Alexandria. They also bear mute witness to a literacy rate reached again only in the 19th century.

With the fall of Rome, posters went into eclipse. The cities became small towns, and most people lived on farms. Very few people could read and write, and most of these were behind monastery walls.

With the Renaissance, learning and literacy revived; so did skills and communications. Craftsmen and merchants posted signs outside their shops advertising their services: the locksmith with a big key, the draper with a huge pair of scissors, the glover with a hand. Then as now, gold was the universal standard of exchange. The Medici, the leading bankers of Italy, hung three golden balls outside their place of business; these were originally part of the family's coat of arms. They have been the symbol of the moneylender ever since. You still see them hanging outside the old-fashioned pawnshop, wherever it survives.

Most distinguished among these early signs is one painted in 1516 by Hans Holbein, the Younger. Like many others of its day, it is painted on both sides, so that it may be seen by people coming toward the door from either direction. It advertises a schoolmaster who offers to teach reading and writing to young and old, burghers and apprentices. He offers proficiency in the shortest possible time, and uses a modern copy writer's high pressure when he says he doesn't want to take money from anyone who shows no aptitude for learning. How he expected to sell prospects when they couldn't read remains a mystery. This Holbein work is now at the Museum at Basel.

By the time young Holbein painted this sign, printing was already half a century old, and engraving was a rapidly developing art. Thousands of people were reading, and printing had become such a big business that the printer-publishers were advertising their books and themselves by means of placards.

Except for tradesmen's signs above their doors, these early posters were still nothing but large sheets, selling by means of the printed word. Printed illustration made its first appearance in 1491, when an Antwerp publisher introduced an early example of sex appeal in a poster advertising his book, *The Lovely Melusina*, with a crude woodcut showing the heroine in her bath.

A poster done by a much better artist, Albrecht Altdorfer, advertised a

Und und zu wissen sey Jedermänniglich : Daß in diese
Statt ist ankommen eine frembde Persohn / mit einem
wunderlichen Thier / ist genannt Romdarius / kombt aus
dem Land von Africa und Asia / dieses Thier ist von dem
Türckischen Kaiser geschenckt worden einem Fürsten in
Tätter-Land / dieses Thier ist 8. Schuh hoch / und 15 lang. Es kan mäch-
tig geschwind lauffen in seinen Landen / das seyn die Thier / die in der
Sand-See ein 50. Meilen lauffen auff ein Tag / auch werden sie gebraucht
auff die Post / sie werden auch gebraucht in Kriegs Expeditionis / die grobe
Stück und Munition darauff zu führen / man schreibt aus Asia / daß sie
3000 Pfund tragen können / es kan dieses Thier in 48. Stunden ohne
Fressen marchieren / und wann es frist / so frist es nicht viel auff einmahl /
es kan auch zu Sommerszeiten 3. Monath ohne Sauffen leben / wann es
saufft / so saufft es viel auff einmahl. Wer nun Lust und Belieben
träget solches Thier zu sehen / der wolle sich verfügen

Carnival poster of a dromedary, Germany, early 17th century

Hie seind zemercken die zeichen der falschen gul
dm im nyderland gemacht · vnd seind etlicher
müntzer zü Göttingen in Sachsen vnd in an
dern stetten verprannt vnd auf vier thurmen
von in gemuntzet ·

¶ Itm̄ die guldin auff d vier herrn
schlegt mit einem czwifaltigen · w ·
das steet oben an dem mentzer vñ
ist falsch ·

¶ Die guldin mit einem apfel auf
einer seytē vñ sant johannes auff
der andern seytē ei ein schilt · mit ey
nem leo · etlich seind falsch ·

¶ Die guldin mit einem apfel auf
einer seyten · vnd die ander seyten
sant Peter mit einem stern an der
prust sölt steen sant johannes auf
den Hainburger schlag ·

¶ Die guldin mit dem bischof mit
einem grossen schilt · vñ obē an dē
handt ein · b · mit einem dittel auff
den kölnischen schlag ·

¶ Die guldin mit einē apffel auff
einer seyten vñ em creücz mit einē
sterṅ die an der seite zwischen den
füssen auff franckfurter schlag seid
etlich falsch ·

¶ Item die vorgenannten guldin ist einer mit besser dann
fünff weyßpfenning · vñ ist der raiff vmbher guldin eins
halben halms dick · vñ das corpus ist gantz küpfferin vñ
übergült ·

¶ Vnd das kupffer ist so hözrt gemüntzet vnnd gesotten
das es wol clingt · darumb mag sy niemād erkennen an
dem clanng oder an dem strich ·

A poster done by a much better artist, Albrecht Altdorfer, advertised a lottery to be held in Rostock in the Duchy of Mecklenburg in 1518. At the top, he shows how the lottery drawings will be made fairly and squarely (no cheating) in full view of the public; the text at the bottom emphasizes this. Then, to stimulate the sale of lottery tickets, he shows the prizes you can win: silverware, furs, a rosary, bolts of cloth. To make doubly sure that these prizes will sell tickets, he gives the cash value of each, just as a modern advertiser does in his prize contests.

One of the earliest posters selling merchandise outright is a French creation. It advertises what was apparently a new luxury in its day: silk stockings.

In the 17th and 18th centuries, posters served new uses: they advertised traveling shows of circuses, menageries, acrobats, freaks, wax works, and performing dogs. Usually the work of printers who did their own engraving, they show little imagination, and only amateur draughtsmanship.

An early example of the concept of mass production in posters is one prepared by a Dutch sea captain in 1747, advertising showings of a Bengalese rhinoceros. The copy is in four languages — Latin, French, German and English — so that the captain could use the same poster to advertise his animal wherever he traveled in western Europe.

Nearly a hundred years earlier, by 1653, posters had already proved so effective a means of spreading propaganda that a French edict prohibited their being printed or posted without royal permission; only publishers and booksellers, a specially privileged class, were exempt. A regulation of 1722 forbade anyone to mount posters in public places unless he was a state-employed bill poster, hired for the purpose, and subject to public scrutiny. This French regulation is still in effect. Although eighteenth-century rationalism produced such satiric flights of fancy as *Gulliver's Travels* and *Candide*, it distrusted imagination in poster art.

A poster of 1715, advertising umbrellas and parasols, shows the merchandise as realistically as the mail order catalogs of two hundred years later. The copy is as exhaustive as that of a Sears Roebuck catalog. Whatever persuasive selling appeared was as feeble and tasteless as the poorer advertising of our own day.

Governments used posters to lure men into their armies by showing soldiers in handsome uniforms. To many an unemployed man, military service meant not merely regular meals and regular pay, but also new clothes he probably could not otherwise afford.

29

American recruiting posters were even cruder. One, dating from the Civil War, shows a buck private holding an enormous American flag, his right foot triumphantly planted over an enemy officer immaculately dressed, and obligingly dead in such perfect repose as to do credit to a modern undertaker. The left-hand background is a homecoming parade; the right-hand, a scene of houses burning, corpses on the street, and people fleeing the devastation of the enemy territory. More copy than is now carried by many full pages offers volunteers good pay, bonuses, survivors' benefits, land grants, and even immediate cash as a reward, or down payment, for enlisting. Patriotism had to be whipped up by appeals to personal greed.

As art, these and other early American posters advertising shows, circuses, etc., are so ludicrous as to make us smile when we see them today. But their flamboyant colors were the result of remarkable advances in printing and lithography which we must examine in detail.

Poster for a pocket umbrella, Paris, 1715

PARAPLUYE DANS LETUY

PARAPLUYES
ET PARASOLS
A PORTER DANS LA POCHE.

LES Parapluyes dont Mr Marius a trouvé le secret, ne pésent que 5. a 6. onces : ils ne tiennent pas plus de place qu'une petite Ecritoire , & n'embaraffent point la poche ; ainfi chacun peut fans s'incommoder en avoir un fur foy par précaution contre le mauvais temps. Ils font cependant auffi grands, plus folides, refiftent mieux aux grands vents, & fe tendent auffi vite que ceux qui fonten ufage.

C'eft le témoignage que Mesfieurs de l'Academie Royale des Sciences en ont rendu.

Cette nouvelle Invention a paru avoir été bien reçuë du Public par le grand debit qui s'en eft fait , ce qui a excité l'Auteur à la perfectionner , au point qu'il ne laiffe plus rien à fouhaiter du côté de la folidité.

A l'égard de ceux qui font ornez , l'on conviendra qu'il ne s'eft encore rien vû en Paraffols de plus agréable pour le goût & la legereté , & que l'on peut contenter en ce genre les Curieux les plus difficiles , pour la richeffe des montures & des ornemens. *Ils auront tous fa marque.*

Ils fe font & fe vendent à Paris chez Mr MARIUS,
demeurant ruë des Foffez Saint Germain ,
aux trois Entonnoirs.

Par l'autorité d'un Privilege du Roy , portant deffenfe par toute l'étenduë du Royaume de le contrefaire , à peine de mille livres d'amende.

Il ne faut pas confondre cet Invention avec celle des Parapluyes dont les branches fe mettent dans une Sarbacanne. Ces fortes de Parapluyes ont deplû par leur petiteffe & leur peu de folidité , d'ailleurs il falloit trop de temps pour les tendre.

TROUPE LEGERE,
A PIED ET A CHEVAL
LEGION
DE FLANDRE
DRAGONS.

DE PAR LE ROY.

ON fait sçavoir à toutes sortes de Personnes de quelle qualité & condition qu'elles soyent, qui voudront prendre Parti dans la Légion de Flandre, n'auront qu'à s'adresser à Monsieur DE PIESSAC Lieutenant des Dragons de ladite Légion, qui leur fera toutes sortes de bonnes compositions. Les jeunes Gens de Familles seront distingués.

Il recompensera ceux qui lui procureront des beaux Hommes.

Il loge chez

1720. (2) FAC-SIMILE D'UNE AFFICHE DE *Racoleurs* (Collection de l'Auteur)

Recruiting poster for the Royal Dragoons, France, 1720

3

LITHOGRAPHY AND NEW FREEDOM

A POSTER CAN BE OF ANY SIZE. A postage stamp is a miniature poster; and a spectacular sign the length of a city block, like those in Times Square in New York, is also a poster.

By the time the Kings of France restricted their use, commercial posters had already proved themselves so valuable that many businessmen found they could hardly prosper without them. Unable because of legal restrictions to use large signs or printed poster sheets, they hired printers and engravers to produce miniature posters that could be distributed in quantity by hand. These were the first business cards.

The French apparently set the fashion for business cards, but they soon became popular in England, too. No less an artist than William Hogarth engraved a good many of these for goldsmiths, drapers, and tailors in London. His contemporary, Francesco Bartolozzi, also working in England, was even more successful; he and his pupils did slick and somewhat overornamented business cards for all kinds of tradesmen, for concerts, theatres, benefits, etc., and even engraved some of the tickets with fancy designs that were, in effect, miniature posters.

In France there was a parallel development: watchmakers, jewelers, perfumers, builders, and even chimney sweeps distributed their artistically conceived business cards by the tens of thousands, and drummed up trade with these miniatures when the right to use large posters in public places was closed to them, or beyond their means.

Around the beginning of the 19th century the French carried this development one step farther; as tobacco, soap and other articles in common use began to appear in packages under brand names, the tiny posters of the business cards were transferred or adapted to wrappers, boxes, and other containers. While they were a far cry from today's meticulously planned packaging, they were an early recognition of the twin facts that:

(a) packages sell merchandise; and
(b) the best-designed packages are usually miniature posters.

Another nineteenth-century development changed the whole approach to poster art and made it a far more effective propaganda and commercial tool then it had ever been. The change came with two improvements in printing. One of these was the discovery of the lithographic process.

Alois Senefelder (1771-1834) capitalized on the fact that oil and water do not mix. In 1795 he applied this knowledge to planographic printing. In his native Bavaria he found a porous limestone (still considered the best material for lithography as an art process), which could be ground to a level surface of any desired texture. The drawing is made directly on the stone with wax crayon or ink that contains soap or grease. This fatty acid interacts with the lime of the stone and forms an insoluble lime soap on the surface, which will accept the greasy printing ink and reject water. After the grease penetrates the stone, the drawing is washed off with turpentine and water. Next, the stone is inked with a roller and printed. The stone must be kept moist during this process.

As a printing process, lithography is probably the most unrestricted of all, producing tones ranging from intense black to the most delicate grays, and sensitively reproducing the textures of the original drawing. Color lithography requires as many stones as the number of basic colors employed.

The consequences of this technique were scarcely realized at the time. Seventy years later artists were to discover that it gave them much greater freedom than engraving had ever done. Where engraving depended on painstakingly subtle gradations of line to create the effects of light and shadow and depth, lithography achieved its effects with large, bold masses of flat color, with quick,

Jules Chéret's unmistakable personal style is seen in this example. One of the earliest lithographed posters in color

suggestive strokes, and with gradations of tone easily produced by variations in the artist's pressure on his crayon.

Meanwhile, another improvement in printing made possible a far wider dissemination of posters; the development of high speed presses. In 1811, Friederich König (1774 (?)-1833) first applied steam power to drive a printing press. Shortly thereafter, in collaboration with another German, Friederich Andreas Bauer, he developed a more practical flat bed press with a revolving cylinder for The London Times, which used it for the first time in its edition of November 29, 1814, turning out 1100 impressions per hour. By 1848, further improvements had raised the speed of presses to 10,000 sheets an hour; and in 1865 the web press raised printing production to new heights by feeding the paper from a continuous roll instead of from pre-cut sheets.

The new speed was capitalized in the United States by an enterprising firm of lithographers, Currier and Ives.

While their fame rests not on their posters, but on their chromos illustrating American life and tastes of their time, I want to dwell momentarily on the mechanics of their operation, because it was by their ingenuity in production that they paved the way to the development of American high speed printing.

With an astonishing nose for news, and with the realization that their success depended on speed and mass production, Currier and Ives organized their operation to an amazing efficiency by rushing their artists to a newsworthy scene, where they could draw on the spot what they saw. Four days after the event, Currier and Ives prints of *Ruins of the Merchants' Exchange* were being sold all over New York.

The earliest Currier and Ives prints were lithographed in black only. They were then colored by hand. When further printing improvements permitted accurate color register, the prints were lithographed in full color by successive printings. A few years after the Merchants' Exchange fire, the steamship Lexington burned in Long Island Sound. Currier and Ives' imaginative recreation of the disaster was on the streets in quantity three days later, with a full description of the catastrophe. During their 72 years in business, this firm turned out over 7000 different lithographic subjects. Quaint and sentimental as these chromos may seem today, they were marvels of execution in their own time. Today, the overelaborate wealth of detail of these collectors' items precludes our considering them as posters; they were merely illustrations. But they showed Europe how to produce lithography in several colors, and how to do it fast.

When these prints and other American lithographs — especially the Civil War recruiting posters — reached England, they attracted the attention of a young Frenchman, Jules Chéret (1836-1932), who was then working as an artist for a London lithographer.

In 1866 Chéret set up his own printing establishment in Paris and created startling effects with three-color printing, then a novelty. An accomplished artist in his own right — he was one of the Impressionists — he set new artistic standards for posters by doing his own drawing directly on the stone with such telling effect that his posters achieved the effect of oil paintings.

But Chéret did much more than create a key place for the artist in poster design, a place the artist has held ever since. He realized also that the primary job of a poster was to *sell*. The liberal use of large masses of color was one way of arresting attention, and Chéret used colors liberally, and in brilliant juxtaposition. Simplification of all elements was another way of driving home the poster's message; and Chéret minimized backgrounds, or dropped them completely, thereby forcing his figures and lettering to dominate his design.

Realizing, too, that you can't be reticent when you're trying to sell something, Chéret gave his figures a vitality no posters had ever had before his time. He achieved this by simplifying his lines, giving them motion and flow, and making his lettering echo the movement of their rhythm. The results were amazing. In his posters for a skating rink you could almost hear the music in the movement of figures and feet. His book jacket for *Scaramouche* is a gay harlequinade; his opera poster a carnival. In today's parlance, he sold the sizzle as well as the steak. No wonder his dancing figures, in their riots of color, gladdened the streets of Paris and drew ever larger crowds to the cabarets, the ballrooms, the theatres they advertised!

Today we can analyze his work objectively. To begin with, there is always *action* in his posters — action so vital and irrepressible as to force itself on the viewer with a power impossible to ignore. His lettering is always clean and legible at a distance, kept away from backgrounds, and in complete contrast to them.

His figures are flat, with little perspective. Only occasionally does he show a complete figure. Even when he does, the absence of a frame suggests a whole world going far beyond the edges of the poster sheet. This, like his color and his vitality, draws in the onlooker as a participant in the composition, and lets his imagination supply whatever elements may be missing, but associated with the subject — music, drinks, gay company in the theatrical posters; a cozy home in a poster for lamp oil; a social occasion in a poster for face powder, and so on.

Whether or not Chéret was conscious of the revolution he created in poster design, he laid down certain principles which poster artists have followed ever since.

First of all, he realized that a poster cannot be overburdened with detail. Second, it should not be too literal.

Third, it must enlist the viewer as a participant. This has since become a basic principle of all advertising, even on television.

Fourth, it must imply a world of continuing action, or enjoyment of the product beyond the confines of the sheet: a poster which leaves nothing to the imagination is not a good poster.

Finally, in the onrush of vitality which is the new dimension Chéret gave to poster art, you have to sell. And what you sell is not necessarily the product, but the *benefits* it gives the buyer: not the oil, but the lovely lamplight it provides; not the skating rink, but the enjoyment it gives you; not the powder, but the beauty it creates.

Today's poster artist who follows these principles can scarcely go wrong.

George Giusti's abstract design in brilliant color for Holiday
made this one of the outstanding poster covers for 1962

40

4

THE POSTER
BECOMES FINE ART

CHERET, LIKE OTHER POSTER ARTISTS OF HIS TIME, learned his effects largely
from Japanese prints. While Japanese prints had been seen in Paris before, it was
apparently an exhibit of them sponsored by Edmond de Goncourt that led French
painters to think of art in new terms, for the Japanese print does what European
artists had never done before, and its radically different viewpoint did much
to determine the character of modern poster art.

A Japanese print achieves a sort of miracle in that it is flat without ever seem-
ing to be just two-dimensional. It ignores relief, sculptured effects, and, in many
cases, shadows—all the things that create a third dimension for the Western artist.
The little modeling it may employ is suggested rather than represented. Perspective is empirical, determined by observation, or even experiment, rather
than by rules or scientific method.

A more basic property of the Japanese print is that its artist gives us not the
surface translation of what he sees, but rather his concept of it. In other words,
he is in a sense an Impressionist; and it is no accident that the first exhibit of
Japanese prints in Europe created such excitement at precisely the time when
the Impressionists and their fresh point of view were beginning to be accepted.
The Japanese prints portrayed martial temper, actors in dramatic moments, frank
gaiety, action, movement, vitality: a personality communicating itself directly
with the viewer.

Action was swiftened or tempered by a brush stroke developed from cal-

ligraphy. And therein lay endless new possibilities for the European artist. At the same time, the elimination or subjugation of backgrounds, the clean, fastidious orderliness of color arrangement, the placing of the subject far into the foreground — all these force and focus attention on the central subject. Because there is little or no background into which the eye can stray, there can be no diffusion of interest.

All these properties are precisely those of the modern poster. It startles the viewer and holds his eye unexpectedly, and for longer than he had intended. It communicates its message directly, simply, dramatically, and completely. It is easy to remember, difficult to forget.

Chéret incorporated these characteristics into his posters. But we must admit that he repeated himself endlessly. While many of the attitudes of his figures may recall those of the rococo period of the *fêtes-galantes* painters of the 18th century — Watteau, Boucher, Fragonard and others — their dress is modern, and their faces . . .

There we come to a significant difference: his faces are tired masks of sophistication that for all their gaiety betray a bitter melancholy. This ultra-sophistication was in the air of Paris at the close of the nineteenth century; and a far greater artist than Chéret portrayed it with such mastery as to make himself immortal.

His name is well known: Henri de Toulouse-Lautrec (1864-1901). An indefatigable painter who developed an amazing objectivity in his observation, he began to create posters in 1891, his first important one for the newly opened Moulin Rouge. This and a few others may seem at first glance similar to Chéret's posters; but more careful examination dispels this impression immediately.

Toulouse-Lautrec avoided the brilliant colors Chéret preferred. Instead, his colors all contribute to the impression of the sickly world he portrayed — sulphurous primrose yellows, tired lavenders, jaundiced greens, faded grays.

His characters are individuals, not types. Drawn largely from the underworld, their faces are those they present to the public as entertainers; yet, amazingly, their individual characters come through: the aristocratic reserve of Jane Avril, the dying embers of hope in the eyes of the acrobat Seduta, the pained

acquiescence of Gazelle. Each one comes to life in his own way; and because they live as individuals on Toulouse-Lautrec's posters, the viewer is intrigued, and wants to see and know them more intimately, to see them in real life wherever they are performing.

Memorable characters, all of them; and Toulouse-Lautrec painted them with a chaste honesty and human sympathy that has immortalized and redeemed them. And whether he knew it or not, Toulouse-Lautrec knew what the cabarets had to sell better than Chéret ever had.

Chéret sold gaiety, even though his faces did not always convey it. Toulouse-Lautrec also sold gaiety to the cabaret customers; but it was intermingled with the depravity they secretly wanted to see. Here, his posters said in effect, are the prostitutes, the drug addicts, the dregs of humanity, all performing for you. They may not be pretty sights, but this is the way they are: give them your francs as I give them my sympathy and understanding. They may be unappetizing, but here they are, human despite their masks, portrayed with all the taste of aristocratic detachment. It was a world far removed from that of Chéret.

Chéret's gaiety was much the same from one poster to the next; it promised fun to everybody. Toulouse-Lautrec's poster of Eglantine's troupe is a close-up of legs and billowing skirts in a dance routine; this is what the customers really wanted to see. Similarly, his poster of Aristide Bruant, the cabaret owner who insulted all his customers, is a view from the back, most of the space covered by a sinister cloak and a slouch hat; only the hand grasping the stick and the leering profile suggest this demonic character. But they are all that is necessary; they tell the whole story, and sell what the public wants to see and buy.

His fame established, Toulouse-Lautrec turned to the art of lithography and in his later posters he drew on the stones, himself. One of these was immense, a single sheet 55″ x 47″. These later posters are such marvels of execution that the surviving prints are almost priceless, for his posters go far beyond those of his contemporaries as supreme examples of the art. He introduced the perspective of the close-up: Jane Avril flaunts her skirts, but we see her through the neck of the bull fiddle in the orchestra. Seduta, legs in black tights and spread far apart, rests tiredly on a red plush divan between acts while a patron propositions a woman in the background. In another poster, a nameless woman, overdressed in the fashion of her day, is coyly considering whether or not to pose for the photographer in the background, whose services the poster advertises. M. Sescau, the photographer, could never have achieved anything like this with his camera.

Another early master of poster art, a Swiss named Théophile Steinlen, was neither as flamboyant as Chéret nor as grotesque as Toulouse-Lautrec. While his posters were as simple as theirs, they were in a quieter and more universal key, and portrayed ordinary men and women in their everyday lives and pursuits. Most of Steinlen's work is a far cry from the decadence of Montmartre's cabarets. He loved cats. His most celebrated poster, for Viengeannes Milk, shows a little girl in a simple red dress which dominates all other colors in the poster. She is drinking a bowl of milk, and three cats at her feet, one with a paw on her knee, are jealously waiting their turn for a taste. Done around the turn of the century, it carried poster art to a height that has rarely been equalled.

One *chanteuse* who captivated Paris just before the turn of the century was Yvette Guilbert. Every artist tried to capture her special magic in his art: Chéret catches her in the profile of a smile inviting the onlooker to share her *double-entendre;* Toulouse-Lautrec did several studies of her, usually in the midst of a song; Steinlen, who shows her uncorseted, as she looked from backstage, gives her more mystery, and fills in his background with a rapt, attentive audience beyond the footlights.

Paris, in the nineties was a gay city. Art was finding a new medium of expression in the poster, and the craze for creating them was infectious. Bill posters, book jackets, song covers, small *affiches* — Daumier, Millet, Manet, and countless other artists produced them, even if only now and then.

One of the most remarkable posters of the time, done by Pierre Bonnard (1867-1947), advertised France-Champagne by portraying an inebriated woman holding a closed fan in one hand and an overflowing glass of champagne in the other. It was this poster that won Toulouse-Lautrec's admiration and led him to become acquainted with Bonnard; but Toulouse-Lautrec was shocked when the artist who had so effectively advertised champagne refused to drink with him!

Lautrec

One of the first of the Gay Nineties posters,
by Paul Berthon. About 60 inches high

48

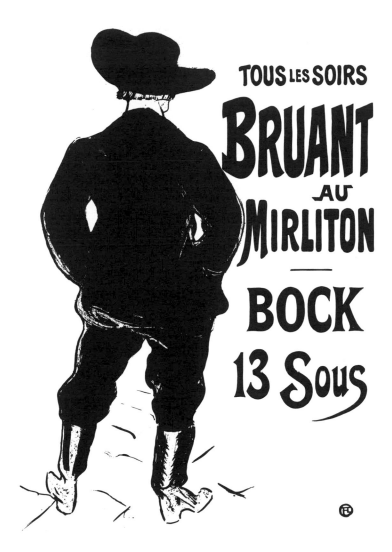

TOUS LES SOIRS

BRUANT
AU
MIRLITON
—
BOCK
13 SOUS

Henri de Toulouse-Lautrec's first poster of Aristide Bruant

Bonnard did one other celebrated poster—a brooding piece of evocation for *La Revue Blanche*. The background is a wall repetitiously covered with other little placards for *La Revue Blanche;* in the foreground a heavily cloaked woman, her face half hidden in the folds of her cape, stares out mysteriously while a leering, grotesque gamin at her left calls attention to her with his distorted finger. The whole poster is dominated by gray tones that heighten its intriguing quality.

A much more intimate friend of Toulouse-Lautrec's, Louis Anquetin, limited his output, like Bonnard, to two posters; but one of these, done as early as 1886, is as immortal as any poster is ever likely to be. The burly son of a butcher, Anquetin had a first-hand acquaintance with grossness; and in this poster he gave it free rein. His celebrated poster shows another Parisian cafe attraction, a fat woman named Marguerite Dufay. Anquetin portrays her in such blatant and boisterous vulgarity that she is positively refreshing. She is loud, ugly and brassy like the larger-than-life size trombone she plays. No poster equals this one for infectious bluster; it invites you to join in the fun as powerfully as if you were right in the music hall hearing Marguerite perform. This creation of audience participation is the test of a great actor; ideally, it should be the goal of every poster artist.

Unfortunately, it was this very characteristic, this urgent immediacy, that vanished from French poster art almost as quickly as it had appeared. Just as Greek philosophy degenerated into medieval dialectic, so French poster art rapidly became so refined and elaborated that it became lifeless decoration.

Eugene Grasset was probably the foremost exponent of this new form. Influenced by Italian Renaissance and Greek artists, Gothic and Pre-Raphaelite British originals, and even by Japanese flower arrangements, Grasset's posters were masterpieces of draughtsmanship, and such tasteful and well-balanced harmonies of color as to suggest stained glass windows. Indeed, Grasset's chief claims to fame are his stained glass windows. His posters are paintings more than they are posters. When he portrays Sarah Bernhardt as Jeanne d'Arc she becomes a lifeless and incredible statue, baring her body to a shower of arrows. Grasset's later poster work degenerated into a cloying sweetness that was as pointless as it was ineffective. Nevertheless he was widely imitated. In his day he had more followers than Chéret.

Freer in style, quite as colorful, and even more masterly in their draughtsmanship than Grasset's were the posters of Alphonse Mucha, a Czech from Moravia who worked in Paris during the 1890's. His dramatic treatment of women's long hair has often been singled out for praise; intriguing and effective as it is in some of his posters, it becomes a pointless obsession in others.

Mucha's Slavic character expresses itself in his liberal use of gold. The highly imaginative cherubs, palm leaves, mosaics and other unexpected background details that invest his posters are the benchmarks of his unique style and underscore his Byzantine influences. Attractive as this is, the Byzantine element formalizes his work and makes his saintly faces so devoid of expression that they seem always to be far away, rapt in meditation or devotion. No wonder, then, that Adolphe Leon-Willette satirized Mucha in a lithograph in which a little shepherdess kneels devoutly in prayer in front of one of Mucha's beer posters!

5

QUEEN VICTORIA'S UNWRITTEN RULES

Since queen victoria's long reign gave England a peace, a prosperity and a world power unprecedented in all history, few of her contemporaries dreamed of quarreling with the conventions and pompously self-righteous tone of her times. Quite the contrary: the social arbiters of her day proclaimed that it was the ideal for British life. It was a combination of prudishness, respect for the proprieties and for established authority, and rigid conformity with restricted patterns of thought, behavior and self-expression. That it had implications of both hypocrisy and snobbery is undeniable. Its obverse was an excessive concern for propriety, coupled with the notion that only established authority could dictate taste. This imposed restrictions on British poster artists which severely inhibited their self-expression. Ultimately it led them to a dead end from which they were not freed until the exigencies of a world war and influences from abroad created a new British concept of poster art.

Since bill posting was not restricted by law in Britain as it was in France, British poster advertising was already so widespread by the middle of the nineteenth century that there were increasing public protests against its use. The protests were not against the quality of its art, as they should have been, for it was unspeakable. Nor were they against the advertising, as they might have been had the objectors been Socialists. The protests were against the *vulgarity* of indiscriminate and unregulated bill posting.

You have to see some of these early British posters to believe their sponsors

51

actually spent good money for such bad advertising.

Warren's Nubian Blacking was advertised by a Negro grinning at his own reflection in a Wellington boot he had just polished. A Lifebuoy Soap poster shows a baby unaccountably asleep in a meadow, protected by a Landseerish dog, who also keeps watch over a wicker picnic basket from which a cake of Lifebuoy Soap sticks out; below the basket, in the lower left corner, is a small copy panel with the headline: *On Guard.* Including the period!

Possibly in self-defense, apparently motivated by a desire to cloak their taste and their selling with the prestige of knighted or accepted names, some British manufacturers began buying the paintings of famous artists to use in their advertising. This raised the artistic standard, but kept the advertising as ludicrous as it had been. In fact, it added pompous smugness by endowing it with authority.

In this way, Pears' name occupies the upper part of a celebrated portrait's mat, and the word *Soap* descends in illegible, interwined (why?) letters down the right side of the mat. Under the portrait is its title and the artist's signature in flourishing script: *"Bubbles," by Sir John E. Millais, Bart., R. A.* The crowning absurdity is not a couple of pears in the right side of the mat—in those days they couldn't leave white space unfilled!—but the word *PEARS* (all capitals) under the fruit, to make sure you won't mistake them for something else. The poster shows the portrait complete with its wide, gingerbread frame.

There was an epidemic of such pseudo-poster art, some of it even swiping Rubens and Rembrandt for advertising purposes. The surprising thing is that this carried far into the 1880's and even later, when its death knell had actually sounded much earlier.

That bell tolled one day in 1861, when London was startled by the first modern British poster, a one-color woodcut by Fred Walker advertising a Wilkie Collins novel, *The Woman in White.* Its only figure is a heavily draped woman stepping out into the starlit night, her right hand closing the door behind her, the index finger of her other hand to her lips, asking someone to the left of the picture to keep her departure quiet.

This poster is as dramatic today as it was when it first appeared. But the

*A typical creation in chapbook
style, by Aubrey Beardsley*

British public was shocked by more than its drama. Think of it: here was an artist who was a member of the Royal Academy besmirching the dignity of the Academy by lending his talents to advertising! Walker himself took quite a different view. He said: "I am impressed on doing all I can with the first attempt at what I consider might develop into a most important branch of art."

True, other posters carried the signatures of Royal Academicians, but they were posters whose art had been created as portraits or other works of fine art; they were released for poster purposes only as a secondary use, after the art had been officially approved in its pure form, for non-commercial showing in high places.

Walker's *The Woman in White,* however, was deliberately created to help sell a book and serve its publisher; it had no life in the proper galleries before it was shown in hundreds of reproductions to the general public. Hence the shock it created among British artists, critics and the general public. Some people approved because the poster was unquestionably art of a high order; others disapproved because its art was being lent to the vulgar purposes of advertising.

Controversy went farther. Some people had such literal minds that they felt cheated when the excitement and mystery of the poster was not fulfilled, because they said it did not illustrate a single incident in the story. (Actually, it did illustrate a minor incident, Anne's departure from the boat house).

This reaction highlights the fact that British poster art of this period derived largely from book illustration. Rossetti and the Pre-Raphaelite school created a vogue for an imaginary classical dignity expressed in the posters of Walter Crane, and of such Royal Academicians as Prof. Hubert Herkomer, Edward Poynter, and R. Anning Bell. They had learned little more about posters from Fred Walker's remarkable *The Woman in White* than the dramatic effectiveness of white against black.

Thus, a circus poster of Walter Crane's, overburdened with badly-arranged lettering above, below, and even in four corner panels, shows a chariot race, split down the middle and framed in two ornate medallions. Charioteers race in the left-hand panel, and a crowd of Olympians eagerly rushes to bestow laurels on them in the right-hand panel: a scene, the poster tells us, "never before seen in London" nor, quite surely, anywhere else.

So powerful was the obsession with monochrome that a new weekly called itself *Black & White.* In its cover design, a female figure, crowned with laurel and

heavily draped from the waist down, stands on top of the world in a frozen and forbidding attitude, and holds up a placard with the name of the magazine. Although the artist, Professor Herkomer, glosses over the details of her anatomy above the waistline, he was nevertheless severely criticized for the *vulgarity* of his creation. Victorian prudishness couldn't tolerate nudes — not even partial nudes, whose nakedness was only implied rather than stated. And most certainly not if the nudes were not redeemed by some pious title like *Truth, Innocence* or some equally righteous or moralistic name to justify or excuse the limited clothing.

How this dread of vulgarity hampered the artist may be judged by the dictum of Walter Crane, the foremost British poster artist of his time: "I fear that there is something essentially vulgar about the idea of the poster unless it is limited to simple announcements or directions, or becomes a species of heraldry, or signpainting... The very fact of the necessity of shouting loud, and the association with vulgar commercial puffing, are against the artist and so much dead weight."

But Paris was too accessible to London; and Chéret, Toulouse-Lautrec, and other French poster artists were too influential for the Royal Academicians and their pseudo-classical posters. Dudley Hardy introduced French concepts with his cover designs for *Today*, and with his posters for *A Gaiety Girl.* He brought a badly needed lighter touch to British poster art by simplifying line and treatment, and making a few spots of color more telling than large masses. At that, his touch is not exactly light; his Gaiety Girls are pretty hefty, and certainly too overdressed to express the spontaneous gaiety they were intended to convey. Apart from introducing a French touch to British poster art, Hardy had little to contribute.

Brander Matthews said this about the difficulties of British artists: "In England the London fogs somehow got tangled in the brush of the poster maker, and the new art, in its translation from sunny France, lost much of its joyous spirit."

It was the decadence of the 1890's that gave British poster art an unexpected turn. The Gothic spirit, already apparent in Fred Walker's *The Woman in White* and in much English fiction, combined with Oriental influences, a macabre imagination, and the decadent atmosphere of the time to produce a completely original artist: Aubrey Beardsley.

His Art Nouveau combines exquisite taste and delicacy of line with simplified composition. His bizarre fantasy deliberately distorts draughtmanship to produce his grotesque effects. "If nature doesn't conform to my drawings, "Beardsley said, "so much the worse for Nature."

His cleverness and his novel point of view are his most arresting qualities; they always make you take a second look at his work. His first poster, for the Avenue Theatre, shows only the head and shoulders and one arm of a woman. Thin outlines suggest her hair, the other arm (of which a slight part shows), and the edges of her dress. But the whole figure is placed behind a spangled curtain

A poster by Will Bradley, showing the influence of Beardsley, dated 1894

parted in the middle to disclose the foreboding mystery of her face.

Beardsley's sickly color schemes were as startling as Toulouse-Lautrec's; his subjects often had nightmarish and diabolical qualities; yet the net effect was invariably more decorative than persuasive. His composition was always tight rather than free, closed rather than open. While his uncompromising style may place his *Bodley Head* poster at the opposite pole from Walter Crane's overelaborate book jacket for Spenser's *Faerie Queen,* both are basically decorations rather than posters because they are essentially static. And every Pre-Raphaelite must have approved of the idealized landscapes of Beardsley's *Savoy* covers, and of the stylized costumes of his women.

Beardsley's many imitators are of no consequence. His influence was felt more in the United States than in Britain, and even here it vanished under the substantial contributions of artists with a better poster sense.

That poster sense appeared suddenly in England in the 1890's in the work of two artists who signed themselves The Brothers Beggarstaff; their names were James Pryde and William Nicholson. They were the first British artists to simplify poster design by reducing it to essential elements and eliminating everything that did not contribute to a single impression. Their work has no extra posies or other decorative elements. Where outlines can be suggested rather than stated, they let the viewer's imagination supply them. Third dimensions are excluded by the simple, flat masses of their drawings. They used color sparingly, but with telling drama: a black-clothed Hamlet contemplates Yorick's white skull against a brown background. The intensely red British costume of the guard in their *Harper's Magazine* poster becomes part of the red background; and the absence of that British obsession, the frame, carries the eye far beyond the edges of the color. The only other colors used are ochre, for the guard's face and lance, and black, for his beard, hair, eyes, shoes, the braid on his uniform, and the outlines of his shoulders and legs. His ruff and hat buckle are simple drop-out whites; and the white panel housing the tastefully arranged and carefully lettered advertising message becomes part of the poster by being framed in the red background and extending itself under the picture to provide a special space for the artists' signature.

This novel treatment should have been completely acceptable to British advertisers and public alike. Most of the figures the Beggarstaffs pictured were dignified men; their cover design for *The Hour* shows a fully-dressed woman of unquestioned respectability. No hint of Beardsley decadence, nor of Hardy frivolity, appeared in any Beggarstaff posters; on the contrary, they were so severe in their treatment as to be solemn, when they were not downright gloomy.

Yet when the Beggarstaffs' work was shown at an art exhibition in sketches for Nobody's Candles, Nobody's Bluing, Nobody's Pianos, etc., it got more comment from critics than it did contracts from advertisers. I can think of at least three reasons for this failure of the Beggarstaffs to get commercial recognition.

First, those advertisers who bought art above the amateur level wanted it to be a *recognized* art, preferably signed by a member of the Royal Academy. For all their talents, the Beggarstaffs were unrecognized beginners, and one of the unwritten rules of British advertising in those days was that you bought it as a commodity, like clothes or jewelry — and whoever wasn't a purveyor to the Crown was just an ordinary tradesman, and unworthy of notice, regardless of his ability.

Second, and much more important, there seemed to be an unwritten rule to the effect that poster art belonged to the world of books, magazine covers, calendars, catalogs, and the theatre; few advertisers thought of applying it to anything else. Posters created for other products were to a large extent advertisements for cigarettes, those decadent smokes that had not yet attained full respectability.

In all justice let me say that it was the British poster artists themselves who enforced observance of this rule, since all their art — even that of the Beggarstaffs — seemed to derive from book illustration, and never got very far away from it until the middle 1920's, when the powerful influence of American advertising, and the need to make advertising justify its ever-increasing costs, finally upset this inhibiting unwritten regulation.

Finally, in the light of what we now know about advertising, I must admit that arresting as many early British posters were, they were not good advertising, because they lacked one all-important ingredient: persuasion. They evoked curiosity rather than compulsion.

That was the third reason for the Beggarstaffs' failure. Their works were arresting as illustrations or announcements, but they lacked the compulsion and follow-through — the *sell* — that would have made them good advertising.

No wonder, then, that poster art declined in Britain before the turn of the century. It couldn't supply even first-rate poster artists like the Beggarstaffs with their daily bread because advertisers did not permit enough persuasion to enter their concepts.

That all-important element in poster art had to come from the country that gave birth to advertising as we know it today — the United States.

6

AMERICA AND POSTERS

THE UNITED STATES has been proclaimed by President Kennedy as "the greatest revolutionary country on earth." This is as true in art as it is in politics. It is particularly true of American poster art, which has borrowed liberally from French and British sources, and later from German and other foreign artists. Yet all its posters have an unmistakably American character which often surpassed their original sources in vigor and effectiveness.

Nor is this all that makes American poster art revolutionary. Americans traditionally disrespect authority. Their flair for improvisation, coupled with the dynamics of their competitive economic system, constantly drives them to improve on everything that has been done, including their own best efforts. They no sooner established styles in poster art than they upset them; and while every style had hundreds of imitators, it was the innovators who made news and wrought changes in poster art as well as in business and politics.

Of course this didn't happen overnight. America's lack of an artistic tradition, its repudiation of rules, its irrepressible spontaneousness, should have been fertile soil for the development of an indigenous and effective poster style. If that style took decades to develop, it was for three good reasons:

First, the very lack of an artistic tradition made early American poster art rootless; its creators floundered around, putting down on paper whatever occurred to them, in any arrangement that suggested itself, and without thought of selectivity. The Civil War recruiting posters demonstrate this.

The Beggarstaff Brothers — James Pryde and William Nicholson — produced one of their perfect collaborative poster designs in this timeless example

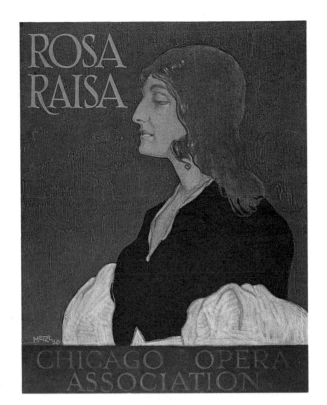

Ervine Metzl re-creates the Italian Renaissance portrait style in this opera poster

The placement of the silhouetted black figure foiled against the familiar background, gives this poster by Ervine Metzl its appealing, nostalgic quality

Second, the success of Currier and Ives created a vogue for telling a story in pictures in such literal, complete, and sentimental detail that early poster artists simply followed their example, and left nothing to the viewer's imagination. Thereby they violated one of the cardinal requirements of good poster creation.

Finally, the early American poster artists were usually German or Czech engravers who made a fetish of literalness, and were more interested in realistic representation than in advertising effectiveness, which meant that they faithfully executed the advertiser's orders, but made no contributions of their own. Thereby they followed advertising instead of leading it, as later American poster artists were to do.

Thus, early circus and theatrical posters were usually highly dramatic presentations of some incident of the performance that would most excite the audience. Their techniques might have come right out of the Currier and Ives shop. Yet they were so widely needed that they were soon syndicated. Lithographers made up posters for popular shows such as *East Lynne* and *Uncle Tom's Cabin*, etc., in quantity, with spaces left blank for the names of the performers and the dates and houses where they would appear; these were simply added in type later. In this way the printers sold the same posters to different road companies who used them wherever they performed. Mechanical considerations, and the need for having posters available anywhere on the continent on short notice, governed what was created and how it was produced. Speed and convenience excluded originality.

It was the immense success of the publishing business that gave poster art a new turn. By the end of the 19th century, universal public education had already placed the United States second only to Japan and the Germanic countries in the percentage of the populace that could read and write. The passion for information of all kinds made American newspapers and magazines proliferate like mushrooms; and while many of them died as quickly as they sprang up, those that survived still numbered their readers in millions. This created a competitive situation without precedent. With so many hundreds of magazines on the newsstands, how could the average citizen decide which one he ought to buy and read?

This was where American advertising and promotional ingenuity went to work. Traditionally, magazines had identified themselves with the public by using the same cover designs year in and year out. In the 1890's some of the British magazines — especially the *Savoy* and *The Yellow Book* — employed artists to create new cover designs; but even these were repeated, and they were basically the same book illustrations that most British posters had been.

American magazines made a clean break with this standard practice by doing two things: first employing outstanding poster artists to create a new cover design for each issue; and second, printing the cover design by itself in quantity (often in enlarged form) for use as advertising posters beyond the newsstands. In this way public interest was aroused and multiplied a thousandfold.

People would seek out the magazines whose cover design posters had intrigued them. *Harper's, Century, Lippincott's, Scribner's* and dozens of other magazines contended with each other for public favor by these competitive means.

Initial efforts by American poster artists to satisfy the voracious appetite of the magazines for new covers were obviously influenced by European craftsmen: Louis Rhead is a simplified Grasset; Will Bradley, a sterilized Beardsley, with improved lettering and over-refined detail. And while the influences of Toulouse-Lautrec, Steinlen, and other Europeans could be seen in the posters of other American poster artists, these artists added new American notes powerful enough to establish a school of their own.

Century Magazine created poster history by announcing a contest for cover designs. To the best of my knowledge, this was the first commercially sponsored art contest the world had ever known. The date: 1895. The contest was given widespread advertising and publicity, and the rewards were sufficient to attract the best artists in the country.

The most outstanding figure among the early American poster artists was Edward Penfield. Influenced by Steinlen, he quickly established a style of his own which combined Parisian chic with London poise and artistic refinement: but all his figures had that clean-cut look which identified them as Americans. They could not possibly be mistaken for Europeans, at least not in their day.

But Penfield contributed more. His action was strong and simple, and well in the foreground of his creations. Non-essentials were eliminated or subordinated. His lettering was always part of his poster, and designed in such a way as to enhance the effectiveness of the whole.

It is especially rewarding to follow some of his posters for *Harper's Magazine* through the years and see how completely each one creates the mood of its particular month, and thus helps sell the magazine by identifying the reading matter with the activities of the prospective customer. A January poster shows a man in Astrakhan cap behind the reins of a horse-drawn sleigh; April, an artist with his sketching materials at the seashore; May, a woman putting two cats out of the house; June, a girl in a straw hat sitting in a rocking chair reading; July, a couple lazing in deck chairs on a cruise; November, another couple at a horse show. In each case the only copy is *Harper's* and the name of the month. Nothing else is necessary.

Robert J. Wildhack went even farther than Penfield in dropping lines, eliminating detail and ignoring backgrounds. In this he anticipates the technique later

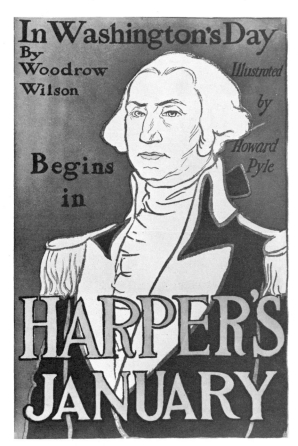

A cover by Edward Penfield
in his typical poster style

Edward Penfield's realistic figure is combined with an impressionistic use of firecrackers to
form the letters of the month

Maxfield Parrish created this appealing, moody poster
for Scribner's sixty-five years ago, and were the magazine in existence today, it would sell its quality content now as it did then. The artist, still alive and
active in 1962, has become a legend in American art.

Here Penfield's illustration tells the whole story

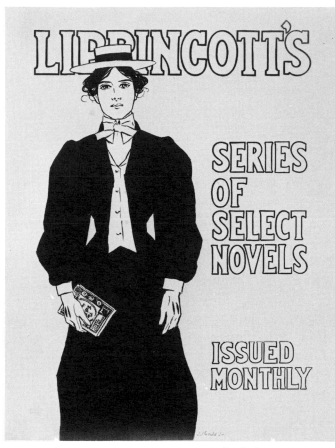

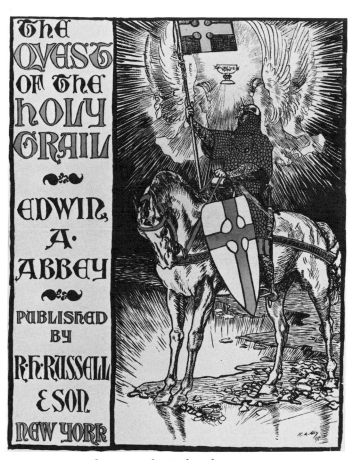

In this magazine poster by J. J.
Gould, Jr., the figure and the
typography are very simplified
— unusual for the period

The strength of this dramatic
illustration by the great mural-
ist, Edwin A. Abbey, is vitiated
by the bad lettering in the panel

perfected in Germany by Ludwig Hohlwein. His sensory impressions are powerful, so much so that he makes you literally feel the sun, the wind, the drowsiness
of the heat, the speed of a Pierce-Arrow automobile. "A poster can give no more
than the 'spirit' or 'atmosphere' of the subject," he said; but later artists were to
show that it could do more: it could sell.

Maxfield Parrish's work went off in another direction. It was original, rich,
bizarre. He had an amazing sense of color, and added many new values to the
poster's spectrum. His detail was elaborate but clean-cut. Yet there was too much
of it to make his work as strong as that of other poster artists of his day.

J. C. Leyendecker was as meticulous in his handling of design as Parrish; but he was more selective, and pointed up what he wanted brought forward by reducing the color values and details of less important elements.

These American poster artists of the turn of the century created posters that gave a larger-than-life effect. This was what made their work so arresting and dramatic, so powerful in its impact. This characteristic was so successful in selling merchandise that it was to remain a basic requirement of effective posters thereafter.

The subjects were unglossed by classical design considerations, or by the new and often affected aesthetic canons proclaimed by some of the European artists.

L'art pour l'art, for example, was shunted aside by American poster artists when it was not completely ignored — which was most of the time. To them, every subject became a symbol of the thing it was selling. And it had to become such a symbol so unmistakably that the buying public accepted it immediately, and for a long time after the original impact. Leyendecker's men in Arrow Collars became national symbols of the well-dressed American male; the women illustrating *That Schoolgirl Complexion* and *The Skin You Love to Touch* became typical of the most desirable American female.

These poster designers achieved their ends by always making the paper a part of the poster; by discovering the effectiveness of white space; by concentrating on an impression rather than on the surface actuality of the subject matter; by regarding the poster as a unit, where every unnecessary frill would be a distraction.

So fundamental were these American contributions to poster art that they affected all poster development from that time to the present. Artists from other countries were to make significant contributions to the styles of poster art, but the essential requirements of a poster — simplicity, directness, impact — become crystallized in the work of Edward Penfield and other American poster artists around the beginning of the twentieth century.

7

THE POSTER
IN GERMANY

Although posters had reached so high a stage of development in France by 1886 that a book was published about them — Maindron's *L'Affiche Illustrée* — they were a medium whose power remained virtually unexplored in neighboring Germany. During the 1890's a few small German posters of note began to appear, especially those of Franz von Stuck; but they were principally announcements of art exhibits. British and French posters for book jackets found little echo in Germany; and the designs for the covers of sheet music, which should have been treated as posters, were simply sentimental and elaborately decorative pastiches of no originality that might just as well have served as book illustrations fifty or sixty years earlier.

It was apparently the stimulus of American magazine covers that roused German artists to create what we might call posters in the modern sense. In 1896 Angelo Jank and Hans Christiansen created some cover designs for *Jugend* that sounded a new note in German art, however archaic and heavy-handed it may seem today.

Jugend and *Simplicissimus* were, in fact, brand new magazines at the time, the former with a somewhat artistic bent, the latter satirical. Both were published in Munich. Because Munich was artistically the Paris of Germany, with conflicting fads, schools and theories, much of this early German poster art was extremely self-conscious.

A completely different and far more original approach to poster creation came from Berlin. Unlike Munich, Berlin had no artistic tradition. Its need for posters was as frankly commercial and competitive as that of New York or Chicago. Consequently these early Berlin posters had far more impact than those created at the same time in more art-conscious Munich. Over and above the more commercial — virtually American — note of these early Berlin posters, they revealed an incisive, original wit for which Berlin has always been noted. Thus, Thomas Theodore Heine, a satirical writer who was also an artist, advertising his talents in the same way the Beggarstaffs had in England — by creating a poster for a nameless product — portrayed a girl in a red dress against a blue background; she is high up on a stepladder, and has her left arm around a giraffe's neck; with her right arm she is trying to wash the spots off the gigantic beast with whatever cleaning fluid she is advertising.

Like the Beggarstaffs, he did not sell this idea, or many of his others, to any advertiser. But a stationer did buy one of his better posters, in which a bottle of black ink has been spilled; out of the spilled ink rises a devil, a white writing quill in his hand. This would probably have sold itself only in Germany, where the legend of Martin Luther's throwing an inkwell at his vision of The Devil is universally known. Heine subsequently created a number of excellent covers for *Simplicissimus.*

I cite Heine because he represents a sort of bridge. While some of his concepts are modern, and take the requirements of poster composition into account, his ideas and his execution are still steeped in the grimness of German legend, and imbued with the heavy-handed *Schwermut* of Böcklin. These and other remote influences, such as those of the Pre-Raphaelites, of Grasset, and of Mucha, also limited the originality and effectiveness of such other German poster artists of the early twentieth century as Otto Eckmann, Hans Unger, Johann Vincenz Cissarz and Fidus; their tightness of concept and technique virtually excluded the freedom a poster must have.

Newer and freer notes were struck — again in Berlin — by Edmund Edel and Julius Klinger. Deliberately stylized and simplified, their posters were both gay and dramatic; by limiting themselves to only a few colors and excluding all superfluous detail, they enhanced the memorability of their work. Thus, Edmund

Edel's poster for *Die Weite Welt* shows a train rushing through the night against a flat gray landscape, suggested in black only by a windmill and a line of trees against the far horizon. Two puffs of white smoke complement the white lettering; the red taillights of the train are like eyes searching the night. Similarly, Klinger's poster advertising a Turkish charity ball shows a dreaming Oriental city in dull blues against a black background, its many minarets punctuating the sky, in which the caricature of a crescent moon, capped by a red Turkish fez, smiles knowingly in anticipation of the festivities.

Making a poster attend strictly to business, so to speak, and making everything in it contribute exclusively to selling what it advertises, reached its ultimate expression in the work of Lucian Bernhard, whose poster for Priester Matches confines itself to two matches and the brand name.

The utter simplification of this poster is something Bernhard himself rarely duplicated, although such simplification was his constant aim. Always concerned first and last with the advertiser's product or message, he avoided everything else. His success was evident from the hundreds of posters he created. Some were translated into French, Italian and English; later he came to the United States, and created the memorable Rem posters in a brand new style.

Two things, however, stood in his way. One was his preoccupation with design rather than drawing. The other was his excessive concern with type. He was an excellent typographer; in fact, the type face he designed is used today throughout that part of the world which uses the Roman alphabet. But frequently his posters are overburdened with excessive copy; and while their typography is always tastefully arranged, it looks better at close range than at a distance.

Here we come to something fundamental in German poster design. European posters are in general much smaller than American posters: some of Bernhard's are only 10″ x 14″; his largest German posters are only 48″ x 36″; only slightly larger than an American one-sheet (42″ x 28″). That is why so many of Bernhard's posters — not to mention those of many other German poster artists — seem to be created more for the printed page, to be seen at close range, than to catch the eye of the casual pedestrian or motorist. Many French and British poster artists of this early period fell into the same typographic trap.

And then came Ludwig Hohlwein.

Hohlwein's creations revolutionized poster concepts and poster art, and had far-reaching influences on other artists both in Europe and in America. Although his first posters were created as far back as 1906, his is still the most famous name among all poster artists.

Hohlwein's unique contribution was not in any one aspect of poster design, but in a bold, unified concept which utilized every element in the poster — line, light, shadow, pattern, color, lettering — to create a single effect. The fact that he was originally trained for architecture may have been largely responsible for this.

His subjects are always well in the foreground, and are usually in bold re-

One of the finest examples of German posters, selling a product by evoking a mood. Designed by Ludwig Hohlwein

Julius Klinger used satire and gaiety to create this sophisticated poster of off-duty officers

lief against a background color, rarely with anything else behind them. His primary, constant and complete concern is with essentials; nothing non-essential intrudes in his posters—which again means that everything in them contributes to create a single, powerful effect. Lines and lettering create repetitive rhythms, often in clothes of checkered patterns. His geometric patterns may be another echo of his architectural training, but he uses them with unforgettable effect. They are underscored in the stances of his figures, even when they are animals.

His lettering is invariably bold and stylized, but always simple, limited and easily read. As a colorist, he is as tasteful as the most celebrated painter; but again, he confines himself to as few colors as he needs, invariably chooses the right ones, and pits them against each other in such a way as to make them completely harmonious, yet individually powerful in contributing just the right element to his total concept.

Particularly interesting is his use of whites, and his utilization of the background color, rather than another tone, to create his amazing distinctions of light and shadow. It is these which help make his posters so dramatic. These, and the fact that his people are always in motion, always doing something, even if it is only taking a drink between billiard shots. By color, by line, by stance, he makes them seem larger than life, the inevitably right expression of his advertising message.

Most celebrated of all are his many posters advertising clothing establishments. He did many of these, yet never repeated himself; each clothing poster is a completely new creation in its own right, and could not possibly be identified with another done for some other advertiser. This means that Hohlwein brought to his poster art a richness of invention, a novelty of message and treatment, that no other poster artist has ever equalled, let alone achieved.

In this timeless poster by Ludwig Hohlwein, the teacups become the focal point, accented by the surrounding black, green and purple-blue

The safety, speed and luxury of ocean travel are symbolized by the smokestacks with the Line's colors. Designed by E. Bauer

All the Winter Olympics have been symbolized by this single figure in the poster by Ludwig Hohlwein

An early poster by Ludwig Hohlwein which laid the foundation for his later style

One would never know this poster by Dietz advertised beer

The snob appeal here would have been more effective had
the artist, H. R. Erdt, used a single large bottle

This design by Lucian Bernhard, in which the product and name tell the whole story, is an object lesson in the essence of good poster art

Ludwig Hohlwein conveys the dependability of the product by his use of the sturdy Bavarian table

In this example by Diez, the barrel, the goat and the pretzel identify the product as Bock beer

Schweiz. Rennverein Sektion Zürich

Pferderennen

Sonntag 21. u. 28. Juni 1925 2ʰ b. j. Witterung
Wollishofer-Allmend.
Preise im Werte von Frs. 22'000.-
Totalisator

*A poster of respectable sociability simplified
in color and design, by Ludwig Hohlwein*

83

Franz von Stuck, a master painter, lent his art to a dramatic poster in black, white, blue and gold

8

POSTERS GO
TO WAR

THE WHOLE WORLD GOT A RUDE SHOCK when the First World War broke out
in September, 1914. Europe had had no major war since 1871, forty-three years
earlier. Such hostilities as the Spanish-American War, the Boer War, the Russo-
Japanese conflict, the Italian-Turkish fracas and the bloody Balkan Wars were
side shows, far away from the sophisticated worlds of London, Paris, Berlin, and
New York. They were of no immediate concern to most of the businessmen who
were relying increasingly on poster advertising for their success. The wars were
of even less concern to the many craftsmen who were creating a new art form in
posters.

After the Germans had swept over Belgium and northeastern France, and
were stopped at the Marne a few weeks after hostilities were declared, the war
settled down to a slow trench warfare. Trench warfare turned out to be a murderous stalemate, but it gave the contenders time and a necessary challenge to
develop new weapons and new concepts of both aggression and defense. Tanks,
airplanes, poison gas—these and dozens of other new weapons Napoleon and
Grant had never dreamed of—were utilized, and ushered in a new kind of war.
And posters became such a useful tool in fighting the war that artists were pressed
into service to produce them in all the major nations. Posters thus acquired new
uses few people had foreseen; and they became more effective than all the patriotic oratory of their day.

The placid world on which war had broken so suddenly was completely

THIS IS THE YEAR!

IT'S UP TO US TO LET 'EM HAVE IT!

Much too much goes on here with the result that the impact is visually lost

unprepared for the catastrophe—militarily, morally, financially, industrially, and intellectually. Recruiting was not the problem it had been in earlier wars, since the contending nations, except for the British and American, conscripted recruits by universal military service; ultimately even the British and Americans had to resort to the draft to get enough soldiers. But there were other new needs for which posters began to be created.

The wisdom of nationalism—and this was nothing if not a nationalistic war—was being increasingly questioned. Pacifism had gained such substantial support in all countries that it could not be ignored. The result was that special recognition and humane treatment were given to conscientious objectors — for the first time in human history on a large scale.

But this left millions of people — especially in the United States — who couldn't quite embrace either pacifism or the horrors of the greatest and most murderous war the world had ever seen. These people, and the millions of opportunists, idlers and slackers on the sidelines, had to be mobilized and regimented; they were needed for work, they were needed in the armed forces, they were needed for every last ounce of moral support in a war effort that was, for the first time in history, totalitarian and world-wide. In other words, the very necessity for war, making it the concern of every last citizen, had to be *sold* to the people. This put all governments into the advertising business; and the principal advertising medium they used was the poster. Posters were cheap; they could be dis-

Russian Poster of the Second World War. Though well designed, it utilizes the technique of the editorial cartoon

*Russian propaganda against the profiteering of the street ped-
dler who is a symbol of capitalism. By Wladimir Lebedeff*

tributed quickly; they could reach everybody; they dramatized their messages with pictures; and they were effective.

The messages of these World War I posters differed completely from those of previous wars. True, before universal military service was legislated, there were appeals to join the British, Canadian, and American forces, and even liberating units (drummed up in the United States) of Czechs and Poles. But most of the war posters had other needs to sell.

Foremost of all was the need for money. The war was still young when all governments faced bankruptcy unless they could pay the monumental costs of battle. War loans in astronomical millions previously undreamed of were advertised wherever space permitted, in every country involved.

But that was only one of many new appeals. Funds for relief and succor, for the entertainment of troops, for the Red Cross, for countless new charities, sprang up overnight. Merchant ships with vitally needed cargoes of food were being sunk on the high seas; and this necessitated repeated appeals for the conservation of food. Clothing was needed for refugees, to whom every discarded rag was a treasure. Books were wanted by the men at the front to take tired minds off their grim duties in their few spare hours. Fuel became as precious as food, and had to be conserved. And — especially in the United States — the urgency and moral righteousness of the war itself had to be sold.

This presented poster artists with problems they had never faced before. There were no precedents for tackling them. It was one thing to create a poster for a theatrical performance or a night club, and not much more difficult to create a mood, via a poster, for a book or magazine. Nor were either of these too far removed from posters like Edward Penfield's associating successful people with a Pierce-Arrow, or J. C. Leyendecker's identifying smart grooming with Arrow Collars. Now, out of a clear sky, poster artists were ordered to create designs that would sell ideas that were catapulted into compulsions by the exigencies of war. They had to sell hate and patriotism, charity and thrift, and appeals for all kinds of help. What was the result?

They floundered. It was easy enough for the French to call their enemies *Les Boches*, and for the British to call them Huns; but names did not create posters, nor did hatred and outrage necessarily give birth to good poster designs. The sinking of the *Lusitania*, the invasion of neutral Belgium, the execution of Nurse Edith Cavell, the victimization of uncounted thousands of innocent civilian bystanders, all shocked the Allies. Many posters dramatized these events; but they were created hastily, with the result that in effect, they were as ephemeral as the average daily cartoon on the editorial page of a newspaper. They recorded the shocking event, but gave neither time nor thought to its imaginative overtones or implications. They were static as a photograph, and almost as rigidly literal. If they intended to corral the viewer's imagination with the horrors they portrayed, they failed — precisely because they lacked the subtlety, the

A famous French poster of the First World War, inspired by the spirit of the French Revolution, designed by Georges Scott

Speed and drive created by a classical silhouette, with text seemingly added as an afterthought, in a poster by Harvey Dunn

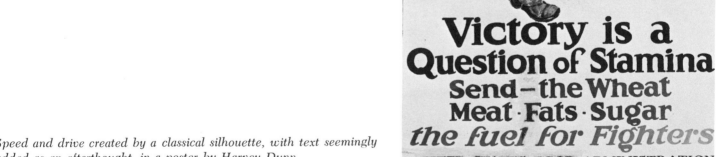

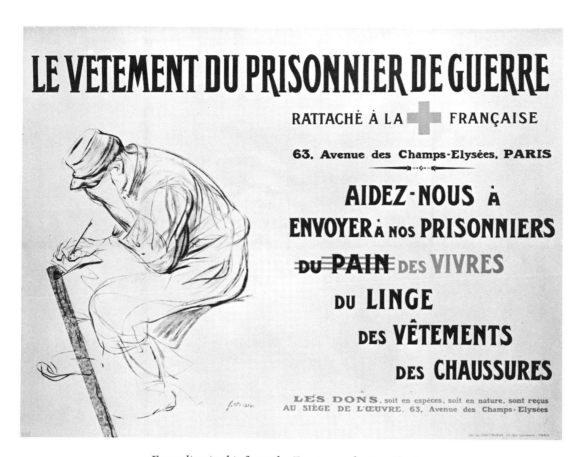

Every line in this figure by Forain emphasizes the impression of loneliness, even the soldier's back turned to the text

artistic finesse, the necessary involvement of the viewer, that could give wings to the viewer's spirit. They illustrated the message; but the message was typographical, and the picture added color without necessarily conveying the compulsion of the message.

In fact, some of them were quite flamboyant, and even pretentious. A Belgian poster, for example, shows a soldier about to fall from a bullet. Alongside him is a grief-stricken woman with a baby, back of him a battlefield, above which Christ rises on the Cross: but between the Cross and the soldier is a shining (though transparent) knight in armor, sword drawn in defiance of all the horror. In retrospect it all seems overdone.

*Frequently cited as one of C. B.
Falls's greatest posters*

BOOKS
WANTED
FOR OUR MEN
IN CAMP AND
"OVER THERE"
TAKE YOUR GIFTS TO
THE PUBLIC LIBRARY

3ᵉ EMPRUNT
DE LA DÉFENSE NATIONALE
CRÉDIT LYONNAIS
Souscrivez

*Another French poster of the First World War
executed in the florid, classical manner*

On les aura!

2ᵉ EMPRUNT
DE
LA DÉFENSE NATIONALE
Souscrivez

*One of France's greatest World War I posters,
gains its impact by a powerful, spirited silhouette*

92

Clever British attempt to identify spades with ships fails because the copy seems to be at variance with the title line at the bottom

Luftſchutz!

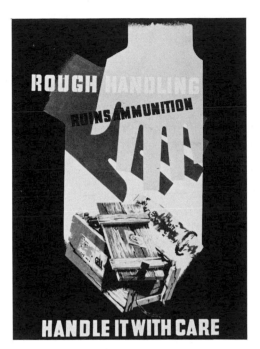

Russian war poster emphasizes
the assembly line where every
man, every link, is important

This British war poster drama-
tizes the situation effectively,
despite its excessive literalness

Russian antireligious propaganda,
identifying the Church with war-
making, tells its story instantly

A powerfully designed Second World War German poster by Ludwig
Hohlwein emphasizes the stance and arrogance of Nazi ambition

Sentimental charity appeal, in which the horrors of war are toned down by the child holding a bandaged doll. Designed by Poullot

Shoot Ships to Germany and help AMERICA WIN—*Schwab*

At this Shipyard are being built ships to carry to our men "Over There"—Food, Clothing, and the Munitions of War.

Without these ships our men will not have an equal chance to fight.

The building of ships is more than a construction job—it is our chance to win the war.

He who gives to his work the best that is in him does his bit as truly as the man who fights.

Delays mean danger.
Are you doing your bit?

Are you giving the best that is in you to help your son, brother, or pal who is "OVER THERE"?

UNITED STATES SHIPPING BOARD EMERGENCY FLEET CORPORATION

MILK THE BACKBONE OF YOUNG BRITAIN

Adolf Treidler's excessive use of type destroys the effectiveness of this poster, although the illustration is in the best poster tradition

A simple English poster by Fitton tells its story directly, without elaboration

The gold coin of France crushes the enemy. The artist utilizes the technique of an editorial cartoon

Harry Townsend used a simulated wood-cut technique for his pictorial element, illustrating perfectly the title lines below

J. C. Leyendecker perfectly reflects the mood of World War I in America in this Liberty Bond poster

The need for united effort makes the worker as much a hero
as the fighter, in this poster by James Montgomery Flagg

It was the same with other war posters. The British, who had never "had" too much love for the French or the Italians who were now their Allies, plastered the British Isles with posters showing a Briton, Frenchman and an Italian united in their forward march to the victory that eluded them for years. Most Italian posters were equally undistinguished, and the French were little better. One notable exception was a French poster by Forain, showing a tired and dirty *poilu* sitting on a crate, wistfully writing a letter home; his exhaustion, filth and ennui are somehow redeemed by his facial expression, at once a longing for peace, and a dream of reunion with the loved ones he left behind.

The war loan posters differed little from one country to the next. Brave soldiers manning battle lines were repeated endlessly; except for the language of the text and the sponsoring government, it would be difficult to tell a German war loan poster from a Russian.

In the United States, where poster art had blazed new paths, the government created a Division of Pictorial Publicity, an official recognition of the importance of poster art. But the Division was in charge of George W. Creel, who understood neither posters nor artists, and assumed that inspirations for the war effort could be bought like bread or coal or steel, and that ideas could be mass produced, like any other needed commodity.

That anything distinguished or effective could be produced under such handicaps was a minor miracle. But it happened. Posters were ground out by the thousands, and reproduced by the millions; occasionally some poster artist rose to the occasion and delivered a poster at once arresting and effective. This was because a handful of them refused to let themselves be carried away by war hysteria, and remembered the job their posters had to do.

Thus, C. B. Falls said flatly and publicly: "A poster should be to the eye what a shouted demand is to the ear." And he made this his guiding principle in one powerful poster after another. One of them, asking people to send their spare books to the local public library for shipment overseas, became one of the most memorable posters the war produced. Similarly, Harrison Fisher's poster for the Red Cross was so effective that its nurse was used for years after the war was over; her outstretched hand is a plea for help directly involving the viewer.

James Montgomery Flagg created what was probably the most memorable of all American posters of that First World War with a picture of Uncle Sam pointing directly at the viewer with the simple caption: *I Want You!* — a direct demand for everyone's participation, in one form or another, in the total war effort.

But these were the exceptions. Most American posters of the time suffered from too much copy; and apparently only one artist, Fred G. Cooper, who was also a type designer, met the problem head on. Cooper did this by eliminating all illustration from most of his posters, and treating the type in such posterized exaggeration that it arrested attention, even when its message was long. It was an effective innovation, harking back to the original posters of ancient times on the one hand, but blazing a new trail by using type as an element of design, and doing it with a new type face which — unlike Bernhard's — seemed specifically designed for poster purposes, and seemed to create a motion or rhythm of its own which actually enhanced the effectiveness of his posters. In this way it created its own pattern of attention, aroused interest by the use of two or more colors and novelty, and focused the viewer's eye irresistibly on its message, even when that message was long and complex.

9

POSTERS BECOME
BIG BUSINESS

FIFTY MONTHS OF GLOBAL WAR left the whole world exhausted, the nations of Europe crippled both in manpower and in their industrial establishments. Of the warring nations, only Japan and the United States came out of the war relatively undamaged; and in the power vacuum left by the battered and bankrupt nations of Europe, the United States became the leading power in the world.

She accepted her new role with extreme reluctance. Isolationism was still so rampant a sentiment in the Middle and Far West that American membership in the League of Nations, which might have gone far toward preventing the Second World War, was voted down in Congress. War had not touched the shores of the United States, and the feverish war effort left many Americans with a longing for peace and an overwhelming desire to get out of Europe and stay at home. The sentiment was typified by Henry Ford. His self-appointed role as a peacemaker in the last year of the war may seem ridiculous now; but in his day he probably had more widespread support than President Wilson.

Henry Ford and the automobile he popularized gave a fresh start to the war-weary American economy. It hastened the postwar adjustments, made a big industrial capital of Detroit, and brought prosperity to an endless chain of kindred industries such as steel, rubber, textiles, chemicals, oil, glass, copper, brass, and countless others. Even more important, it put America on wheels, and gave a new prosperity and the means of transcontinental transportation to millions who previously could scarcely have afforded a horse, let alone a buggy. And it revolu-

Herbert Leupin graphically states that all the news comes with the morning coffee

Utter simplification of two flat colors, combined with fine lettering, makes this poster by Fred G. Cooper a masterpiece

tionized the entire pattern of American living, taking everyone away from home and out on the highways to places they had never dreamed of visiting.

The automobile gave birth to countless new kinds of businesses: gas stations, hot dog and soft drink stands, tourist homes, automobile agencies, drive-in theatres and restaurants, amusement parks, roadhouses, garages and repair shops. To survive, these new enterprises had to advertise. What better place to advertise them than on the highways where they were located? And how do you advertise on highways, if not with posters? Even a slow driver going 20 miles an hour couldn't read an advertising message that wasn't reduced, as posters are, to an absolute minimum of copy and picture: a fast but memorable impression.

The results were both chaotic and pathetic. Signboards and posters of all kinds began cluttering the highways, in all shapes and sizes, in all sorts of locations. Misspellings, bad grammar and inept art flourished — sometimes even on posters sponsored by local communities and police. In the fierce competition of all this homemade art for public attention, the net result was that almost none of it was worth a second look.

However, the opportunities the newly populated highways offered to national and large local or sectional advertisers began turning many a shambles of highway advertising into more orderly, dignified and effective posters selling important new products. Enterprising firms went into the outdoor advertising business all over the country.

Since time began, posters had been of all shapes and sizes. In Europe, they were posted on whatever convenient wall or hoarding offered a blank space, often without the property owner's permission. But even before the First World War, order was brought out of advertising chaos in America by making the 24-sheet poster (104" x 234") the basic unit. This enabled advertisers to produce a single large poster design in quantity, and have it appear simultaneously in hundreds of locations, in all parts of the country.

At the same time, the large outdoor advertising firms usually made it their practice to lease and pay rentals for the land on which they erected their poster panels; this empowered them to remove countless miscellaneous signs and impediments that stood in the way of their own posters. The frames of the poster panels were usually painted in a pleasing green; and in many cases the areas surrounding the 24-sheet showings were attractively landscaped, especially if they were illuminated at night. Obstructions to long-range visibility were also removed, to give the 24-sheets maximum impact. Open boards, that is, unrented poster spaces, were filled with public messages to keep the location attractive and public attention constantly at a maximum. Public interest was further stimulated as advertisers were encouraged to change their posters and their messages once a month.

All this proved a new boon to advertisers. Economies in poster production enabled them to devote added time, money and care to the art work that went into their posters. Standards of art and lithography were perceptibly raised. A little brother of the 24-sheet poster, the 3-sheet (42" x 84") was also standardized, and posted on the walls of retail stores in home neighborhoods. Car cards, appearing in street cars, buses, subway and elevated cars in the larger cities, proved equally effective as posters; and 2-sheets and 1-sheets provided still other poster spaces on station platforms of the subway and elevated lines of Boston, New York, Philadelphia and Chicago, to say nothing of the many suburban railroad lines. After all, size is relative; a car card or point-of-sale display poster seen at a distance of a few feet is just as effective in delivering its message as a 24-sheet seen from a range of several hundred feet. Their shapes and sizes may differ; but the basic requirements of poster creation are the same: to create a startling effect that will arrest the eye of the unwary public, hold it long enough to register its message, and make that message so telling that it will be remembered and make a sale for the advertiser.

Poster advertising organized on such a nation-wide basis gave poster artists an opportunity they had never had before — that of having their work seen by millions of people, clear across a continent. This proved to be an immense stimulus, even though much of it went into misdirected channels and produced indifferent results. But it helped dissipate the doldrums of the years immediately following the First World War. And while outstanding poster artists like the Beggarstaffs had found it extremely difficult to sell their talents to advertisers only a couple of decades earlier, poster artists were now sought out, well paid, and given a chance to work on a far wider variety of subjects and products than they had ever hoped for.

In this new boom, another new business came to the fore to assist both advertisers and artists: the advertising agencies. In many instances, they did not design posters, nor even handle their placing. (Many advertising agencies were curiously blind to the magnetic power of posters, and some of them still are.)

One of a magnificent series of posters for this product employing photography. Designed by Ralph Cowan

A photographic poster, designed by Al Murphy, in which the eye-path is unmistakable and the message instantaneous

Even where the agencies did not create or place poster advertising, their collateral advertising in other media influenced and often dictated poster content; and their art directors set new high standards of performance.

Advertising agencies had existed before the 1920's. But through the genius of men like Albert Lasker, O. B. Winters, Earle Ludgin, John H. Dunham, and others — concentrated, somehow, in Chicago — they made themselves and their agencies responsible to their clients in ways their predecessors and competitors had ignored or shirked. They felt they had a double duty: first, to employ the best artists money could buy, and use them in all their advertising; and second, to leave nothing undone that would make every advertisement — and every poster — produce sales.

This meant centering the whole advertising effort around the right message; and this in turn meant the beginnings of copy analysis and copy research as we now know them. In posters, this sometimes produced too much copy for telling effect. Fortunately, Fred Cooper, whose war posters I have already mentioned, had shown that even long copy could be handled when the lettering became a focal, rather than an incidental, part of the design concept. He now carried his virtuosity even farther in a poster he created for the Fifth Avenue Theatre, where

107

Fred G. Cooper employs an adaptation of the Oriental style in a theatrical poster for the Fifth Avenue Theatre, New York

Isao Nishikima has drawn on his country's traditional conventions to create a striking modern poster

Who could resist the message? This whimsical design by Frank Johnson is perfection

a Japanese dancer was giving a recital performance. He showed the dancer on the left, and a single column of copy, in Japanese script, on the right. The only copy in English was the name and address of the theatre. This poster aroused such curiosity and interest that the dance recital, originally scheduled for only five performances, ran for many weeks.

Centering the poster around the message became more important than ever as artists and agencies had to create posters for all kinds of new products to which the automobile and the boom of the 1920's gave birth: tires, refrigerators, washing machines, batteries, vacuum cleaners, radios, gasoline and oil, motion pictures — to say nothing of old established products and business services that had never used poster advertising before, and now turned to the poster as a powerful medium for making new customers: coal, soap, cereals and other foods; paint, cigarettes, candy; banks, florists, life insurance companies. Poster advertising had never enjoyed such a boom in all its history. Prohibition provided a further stimulus by fostering the soft drink industry, which became one of the largest

A three-stage poster done in comic strip style by Cassandre so successful that it has become the trademark of the product

and most consistent users of poster advertising, and has remained so ever since.

This immense proliferation of advertising, and especially poster advertising, sometimes created difficulties we can now see in retrospect, although neither the artists nor the advertisers were aware of them when they were creating their designs. Chief of these was the fact that the copy sometimes said one thing, the illustration another. To understand how this happened, we must remember that almost until the First World War, most poster advertising was still confined largely to announcements of new publications and cultural or political events such as plays, expositions, circuses, elections, calls for army or other war volunteers, etc. Where posters had been used to advertise merchandise, they did it by association.

Thus, J. C. Leyendecker established an air of social status by showing a couple in evening dress about to get into their chauffeur-driven Pierce-Arrow limousine: snob appeal. Willette had created an overdressed Dutch waitress to associate the Dutch origin of the manufacturer with Houten's Cocoa; National Biscuit Company associated Niagara Falls with Shredded Wheat because the factory was located nearby; if we wonder today what the waterfall had to do with selling you the product, let us reflect that a remnant of it still appears on the Shredded Wheat package.

Maxfield Parrish went similarly far afield in his poster showing three Stone Age people before a fire to advertise Edison Mazda light bulbs; the old obsession for titles and labels survives in the framed words *Primitive Man* which appear at the bottom of the poster.

How silly a poster could become where it relied on association of the illustration with the product is exemplified by a job J. C. Leyendecker did for Ivory Soap. In it a man in a white bathrobe stands solemnly in front of a white bathtub, whose brass handles are gripped in lions' teeth. A white towel is over his arm, a cake of Ivory Soap in his right hand; steam rises from the bathtub and leads up to the word "Ivory," set against a background of terra cotta mosaic. But by having the man's head circled in the "O" of the "Ivory," Leyendecker creates the effect of a halo; and this, coupled with the man's sanctimonious pose and expression and the white robe, makes him look like a Dominican monk, and possibly even a saint, all for the glorification of Ivory Soap.

Sometimes there was little or no connection between the picture, the product and the advertising message. Thus, a Leon Gordon poster has as its subject a statue in an art gallery; only one of the four people in the foreground is actually looking at it; the copy reads "A Modern Masterpiece" and shows the trademark of Hart, Schaffner & Marx Clothes. The statue could scarcely symbolize Hart, Schaffner & Marx Clothes, since the sculptured figure is dressed in a cutaway coat, which was pretty "old hat" by 1917, when the poster appeared.

These and other shortcomings of advertising now led the advertising agencies—especially in Chicago—to make it their business to blend concept, copy

Herbert Leupin's fast communication of
the product in the gloved hand projects
a sensual and a luxurious connotation

Ryuichi Yamashiro has contrived a fine
contrast between the old and the new to
project the modern chair in larger scale
and striking color

and art into a single unified whole. A beautiful woman's face, seen close up, suf-
ficed to convey *The Skin You Love to Touch* for Jergens' Soap; another woman,
similarly treated, sold *That Schoolgirl Complexion* for Palmolive Soap: both had
reason-why copy that sold the product by telling what it did for you. By far the
most memorable poster of its day was Burr Griffin's creation for Fisk Tires: a
little boy on his way to bed, dressed in a long white nightgown against a dark
background; he is carrying a candle in his left hand, and a tire on his right shoul-
der; the copy limits itself to a pun in three words: *Time to Re-Tire*. This 24-

A perfect poster designed by Roy McKie where exaggerated move-ment, spirit, color and humor all combine to form an eye-stopper

The gold and purple color scheme here commu-nicates the sound as well as the mood of music

Simple, classic design emphasizes the power of industry and the dignity of the Swiss Fair

Thomas Derrick has reduced his linear design to absolute essentials in creating a symbol of its message

sheet poster may easily have had the longest life of any billboard advertising ever created; it was used for years afterward.

The posters of the 1920's were not always that successful. Once sex appeal was introduced into advertising, it was overdone, with the result that many a pretty face or female figure was used to sell a product where sex appeal had no legitimate or logical place—merely on the theory that a picture of a beautiful woman would arrest attention. This overblown theory was vulgarized in the more popular forms, especially in calendar art.

Copy was similarly overdone. A William Oberhardt 24-sheet poster reads:

FATIMA

a sensible cigarette

"just enough Turkish"

20 for 25¢   —that's why

The man in the wing collar and bow tie at the right, obviously enjoying the fragrance of his cigarette, is well done. But why the quotation marks around *just enough Turkish?* And why the redundancy of *—that's why?* Copy writers as well as artists had not learned where to stop.

They learned to stop at a single word in the posters for Dodge Bros. automobiles, which even dispensed with illustration, and were produced at low cost by being printed in only a single color. Copy was sometimes limited to a single word such as *Dependable,* centered in white lettering against a blue background, with the Dodge Bros. logotype in the lower right-hand corner. Packard made the most effective use of this technique with its celebrated line, *Ask the Man Who Owns One*—six one-syllable words whose selling impact was inescapable.

And then, suddenly, the heady poster and advertising boom of the 1920's came to an abrupt end with the stock market crash of October, 1929, and the years of depression and large-scale unemployment that followed. In the debacle, poster artists suffered more than advertising, for several reasons that had nothing to do with the still sure-fire effect of a good poster.

Before we examine the drastic results of this on American poster creation, let us see what was happening to posters in Europe.

10

POSTERS COME
BACK TO EUROPE

ONE OF THE ANOMALIES OF EUROPEAN POSTER HISTORY is the gap of thirty or forty sterile years which separates Chéret's ascendancy from Hohlwein's. In the United States, the gap was filled with an enormous upsurge of poster activity and development; but in most of Europe, there were very few posters that rose above a dead level of mediocrity.

For this there were several reasons.

One reason for the lag lay in the fact that advertising had no such meteoric development in Europe as it had in America. While American advertising agencies began to establish branches in Europe in the 1920's and 30's, they had nothing like the success they had in the United States. Often they were little more than brokerage affiliates, or one-man offices built on hope rather than billing. Europeans were not educated to the need or importance of advertising in the American sense until the late 1930's.

Second, when a few courageous European advertisers did venture into poster advertising, they did not do it with the gaudy directness of American poster art. They still treated advertising as a calling card rather than a means of persuasion; an announcement rather than an advertisement. Even in Hohlwein's posters, it is only his art—not the copy—that raises them above this level of business formality, and gives them the dynamic quality of making the name of the advertiser or the product mean something the customer really wants.

Third, we must recognize that successful as Chéret and Toulouse-Lautrec may have been, their more flossy successors, such as Grasset and Mucha, were even more successful, and had many more imitators. Not because they were better poster artists. Quite the contrary: because their art wasn't as violent, novel, or uncompromising as that of their predecessors. They were willing to make concessions to public taste Toulouse-Lautrec wouldn't have tolerated: over-elaborate detail, studied sweetness, dizzying mosaics of pattern and color, tableaux-like, unrealistic attitudes in their frozen figures. This catered to the Victorian stodginess of the mid-nineteenth century, which still governed the artistic taste and commercial reticence of early twentieth century advertisers on the Continent as well as in Britain. Far from advancing poster art, these compromises crippled it. Decoration and reticence are static; poster art is dynamic.

Finally, the early masters — Chéret, Steinlen and Toulouse-Lautrec — were so engrossed in what they were doing, so excited by the possibilities of the new art form they were creating out of the necessities of the moment, that they did not take time to formulate the basic principles of poster creation that expressed themselves so eloquently in their work. The masters themselves sometimes abandoned or ignored their own principles. Only the courageous Beggarstaffs seemed to realize that poster creation imposed severe limitations on the artist, that he had to work within these limitations, but that, once cognizant of them, he could make the most of them, and utilize them to do his bidding. But in their day the Beggarstaffs had little recognition, and less following. Not until Hohlwein came along did any other European artist seem to be completely aware of what you could and could not do with a poster. And Hohlwein's influence was almost 20 years making itself felt in its effect on the work of other poster artists.

Keep it simple must be the poster artist's First Commandment. All superfluous details, and particularly all gratuitous decoration, must be scrupulously excluded from the poster area. Too many European artists yielded to the temptation to make their posters perfectly balanced compositions by adding elements foreign to the central message.

From this follows the second requisite: *that everything on a poster has to be concentrated in a single message, and contribute to a single effect.* Hohlwein's poster for Marco Polo Tea, for example, conveys the warm, dark mystery

Cassandre's dominant prow sells solidity, size, luxury and excitement — everything the magnificent ship connotes

Modern poster treatment for travel that
sells sunshine, shade, sailing, and beaches
abstracted to form an arresting design

The realistic figure in the opu-
lent chair conveys luxury,
while the tubular surroundings
sell the London Underground

Cleverly created by using paper cutouts of different colors,
this poster by Rabajoi immediately conveys its message that
everybody — husband, wife and waiter — all read Paris-Midi

DURHAM·BY·LNER
IT'S QUICKER BY RAIL

This large-scale poster by Frank Brangwyn was done on the stone in color lithography — a singular achievement difficult for contemporaries to duplicate

of the East in his subdued colors, the black, blue and green so nearly in the same sombre key, the Eastern note emphasized in the lone figure of the Oriental serving the tea. No words beyond the name of the product are needed; none were added. Or are furniture, background, or any of the ordinary appurtenances that realistic treatment would demand.

Which leads us to the third requirement: *stark stylization.* Not because a poster artist has to subscribe to what we call modern art — we shall see here that he doesn't — but because his message is *not* addressed to art buyers, art collectors or academicians. He talks to the artistically insensitive, the aesthetically unsophisticated millions who will consume whatever it is he is advertising, and make that advertising pay off. They will not judge his poster as art, or even as

123

advertising. In fact, they won't judge it at all. They may not even be aware that it exists, until they see it repeated often enough. Meantime they may have reacted favorably to its message, but completely on a subconscious level. If that under-the-surface reaction makes them buy the product or service, the poster is a success, no matter how art critics may judge it — or even ignore it.

This leads us to the fourth requirement. Whatever is said has to be said boldly and swiftly, in big masses of color, in as *few* colors as will do the job, and with the lettering helping to convey the message in a flash by becoming an indispensable element of the basic design. *A poster has to sell*, and it has to sell so fast that the viewer gets no chance to change his mind. And so boldly that he won't want to.

Finally, the poster artist must involve the viewer, lead him into the poster, and instantly make him enjoy, or accept without question, whatever it is the poster is selling. In other words, *the poster must convince*. Relatively few European posters between Chéret's day and Hohlwein's met all these requirements.

After the First World War, business in Europe became more competitive than it had ever been. Yet somehow the best European posters did not reflect this, while the worst ones made a mess of it, considered both as art and as advertising. Competition might be as bitter as it was in America—and often much dirtier —but the advertising which presented the face of European business to the consuming public was still wrapped in Victorian reserve. American advertising might be successful in making sales, but many Europeans regarded its boldness and violence as being in bad taste.

It is consequently no accident that when good posters finally emerged in Europe above the morass of artistic compromises in which they had been bogged down since the 1890's, they were subdued in tone, much as the European landscape and the hues of European cities are gentler than those of their American counterparts.

It was Frank Pick, head of the Advertising Department of the London Underground, who turned European poster advertising into new channels, and gave it a new and uniquely British character. Pick recognized the importance of engaging the best artists he could find to sell the services of the London Underground Railway to the millions of Britons who used the dark, crowded subway system every day.

What did he sell them with his posters? Surely not the convenience of subway travel; the customers were using that every day not because they enjoyed it, but because it was the quickest and most convenient way to get to and from their jobs. No; Pick wanted them to use the Underground to lead them to other and more charming gratifications, at times outside the rush hours. By plastering the boards of station platforms with posters of the peaceful English countryside outside London, he invited the customers to use the Underground on weekends and holidays to get away from the crowded city and breathe the fresh air of

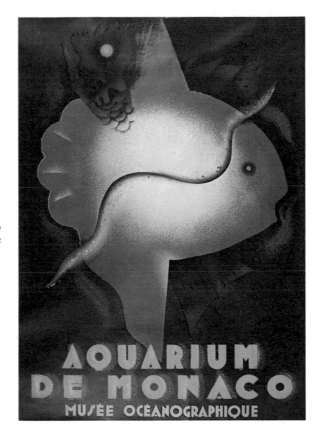

Jean Colin catches the beauty and mystery of underwater life by his consistent use of fluorescent color

A dramatic use of color and facial expression clearly convey the character of the opera advertised

PUBLISHED BY THE SPANISH STATE TOURIST DEPARTMENT, MADRID

SPAIN

Typical example of the overdecorated, overdesigned British poster, depicting a procession of carnival figures against a deep space background

Sunlight and space conveyed by extreme simplification of all elements, by Guy Georget. The original color tells you it's Spain

the open country, the sea and the hills, the meadows and the gardens. In addition, his posters invited them to relax in the city's parks in good weather; and when the countryside and parks were uninviting, his posters suggested they get acquainted with the glories of British heritage housed in London's museums, or attend concerts and theatres.

Thus, Gregory Brown's poster of Little Hampden was for many riders a glimpse into another world, yet accessible by the Underground. Edward Bawden's poster took them into the greenery of Regent's Park; significantly, this poster was one of the first to use sans-serif type dramatically. An exquisitely executed butterfly by Austin Cooper was such a surprising note in the subways that it could not fail to arrest attention: it was only one of the many interesting exhibits awaiting the traveller at London's Natural History Museum. The gaunt trees of Richmond Park were never so tellingly portrayed, or so mysteriously alluring, as in the poster Dame Laura Knight made for the London Underground.

In short, Pick used the London Underground posters to sell travel, even if it was only travel by Underground.

Using posters to sell travel was not new; Western railroads had used travel posters for years in the United States and Canada; but they sold their services by showing the giant redwoods of California, the stupendous sweep of the Grand Canyon, the gigantic splendors of Yosemite and Yellowstone, Glacier National Park and Banff. Everything was on a colossal scale, possibly thanks to Hollywood, possibly because the grandeur of the American West could not be advertised as being anything but the breath-taking, awesome immensity it is.

Certain Transatlantic steamship lines had also used posters to sell travel; but they did it largely by showing ships sailing into the distance, with longing eyes following them. It was the ship that was sold, not its destination. Nostalgia, not travel. And when travel advertising first appeared in Europe it was Swiss, selling the monumental scenic wonders of the Alps.

Against this background of naturally spectacular advertising, and against the blatant violence and directness of American posters selling consumer goods, the London Underground posters struck a brand new note. Simple in design but beautifully executed, they were the first European posters since Toulouse-Lautrec to use fine art commercially, and to use it successfully. They sold quietude and human interest, not spectacles.

The gentle persuasion of these London Underground posters may have done much to open the eyes of British advertisers to the possibilities of poster advertising. E. McKnight Kauffer, an American who produced many of the London Underground posters, was utilized by several other British advertisers, and created (among many other posters) an outstanding campaign for Shell Oil.

This new British trend found an echo across the Channel in Nathan's poster advertising Paris for the French National Railways, though it is less effective than those of the London Underground. But there were other influences at work in France.

The utter simplicity of many American posters and—more dramatically—those of Ludwig Hohlwein—gradually displaced in French posters the meaningless and ineffective repetitions of the styles of Grasset and Mucha. Carlu, Colin and other artists brought new freshness to French poster design while retaining a basically French flavor.

All these were long steps in the right direction. A bolder step was taken by Cassandre. His French Line poster for the then new liner Normandie—later so tragically burned and wrecked at her New York dock—is one of the memorable travel posters of all time. Cassandre does not try to show the ship, or her luxury, or her speed, or any of her other appurtenances. The viewer is treated to a worm's-eye view of her immense bow, rising perpendicularly almost to the top of the poster sheet, the ship's superstructure literally dwarfed above it. All the poster sells is 80,000 tons of ship—what was then the world's largest ocean liner, with all the speed, luxury, comfort and pride of being on the passenger list which the very name of the well-publicized Normandie implied.

Cassandre's great virtue is his utter simplicity, which thrusts what he has to say far into the foreground, and drops everything else. Even such an unpretentious poster as the one he created for Maison Prunier, a restaurant specializing in sea food, shows only a fish, a lobster and a conch, one above the other. But they are supported above a pristine white tablecloth, which is even farther in the foreground than they are, and sells the notion of their being served in a restaurant. Nothing else is necessary but the restaurant's name.

In this poster we see a new influence at work: that of the Bauhaus.

The Bauhaus began as an architectural school in Germany in 1919. It turned its back on established concepts, and promulgated the theory that an edifice could be built up out of units, as a child builds with building blocks; that these could be combined in any number of ways to give structures more variety, more light, more exposed surfaces, with interesting connecting galleries, inner courts, etc. The Bauhaus also experimented with materials that had not been used structurally before: aluminum, glass, poured concrete, bronze.

The Bauhaus went farther. It designed furniture, found new art forms in collages, designed textiles, experimented with abstract painting and new sculptural materials, and even designed type faces. Ultimately—nearly twenty years after it was founded, and after Hitler had closed its operation in Germany—it began to influence poster design, too.

We see this at work in Cassandre's poster for Maison Prunier. Here the elements of the design are virtually abstractions of the subject matter; but instead of being composed, so to speak, they are built up, unit by unit, almost in the manner of Bauhaus architecture.

Ever since Braque, Picasso, Miro and others had broken subjects into their planes and elements and rearranged them in novel relationships to each other, cubism had been a method practiced by more and more painters. Its novel viewpoint toward subject matter was forcefully expressed by so many artists that an ever-widening public responded to it. By the late 1930's it had found its way into poster art, too. Cassandre was only one of the French poster artists who reflects the influences of *Les Fauves.*

Cassandre's most celebrated poster is the one he created for Dubonnet. In fact, it has become Dubonnet's trademark. Influenced partly by cubism and other factors in the new surrealistic art, partly by a brand new art form, the motion picture cartoon, Cassandre's original design for Dubonnet was a three-stage poster, as shown on page —. That only one of the three stages survived and remained fixed in the popular mind as the symbol for Dubonnet is immaterial; it was a bold experiment in adding drama and movement to the single poster concept, and it actually gained power by its repetition of the poster figure in the same size, position and color, the only change being in what the figure was doing with its hands and mouth. Many other posters were to use the two and three-stage technique, some few even a four-stage presentation, in the years that followed.

An obscure American artist, whose very name has been forgotten, created a similarly memorable three-stage poster around the turn of the century. It was only a counter card for barber shops, but it is still remembered, and often cited, in advertising journals. It advertised Newbro's Herpicide, a hair tonic that has all but vanished along with the artist who created its unforgettable advertising. The poster simply showed a gentleman, in the most rudimentary outline, combing his hair. On the head at the extreme left he still has a few hairs to comb; on the next head he has fewer, on the one at the right none at all, being reduced to complete baldness. The copy says starkly "Going—going—gone. Newbro's Herpicide might have saved it."

This then demonstrates the power of a simply presented advertising idea, misleading though the poster may be with its implication that Newbro's Herpicide would prevent baldness. Newbro's may be forgotten, the artist's name is in limbo, but the drama of the poster's simple story lives on.

A London Underground poster recalling the format of Puvis de Chavannes,
that sells the delights of summer idyll without the need of any lettering

Violent perspective made slick by
the airbrush technique, emphasizes railroad dependability in
this poster by Paul Masseau

Lettering placed above and below this striking portrait by
Andrew Johnson, unifies the
message and focuses attention
on Britain's first railroad man

When the artist plays too cute with his lettering for design's sake, it often becomes difficult to read quickly, as in this confusing example

This imaginative and simply presented poster by T. Trepkowski, creates the mood of music and what it evokes when it's Chopin

NÜRNBERG

All the spirit of Nürnberg before World War II is dramatized in this striking vignette impression by Schillinger

A poster by Herrick, well designed, but failing to a degree, since it is difficult for the observer easily to identify the small-scale orbs that note particular stations of the Underground

Another example by Herrick of classical elegance in layout and design for the Underground

Bourbon elegance conveys the re-creation of past glories in the festival it advertises, by Guy Arnoux

The simple village corner symbolizes all the old English towns that can be reached by the Southern Railway. Designed by Gregory Brown

136

Czech poster combining the simplicity of childlike drawing with modern sophistication

The legend tells the story immediately and the characterful illustration supports it perfectly in this arresting poster by Fred Taylor

A restrained and delicate background of grayed colors heightens the bold, dark pattern that rhythmically binds the design

Realistic book illustration, fine in itself, if often too detailed
for instant communication. In this example by R. W. Sullivan,
the total message is lessened by the hard-to-read italic script

A remarkable achievement by Baumgarten, monumental in character and sculptural in concept. Produced in a single-color printing

11

POSTERS BECOME INTERNATIONAL

CUBISM, SURREALISM AND OTHER MODERN ART CONCEPTS had just begun to make their way into European posters when their further development came to an abrupt halt. Hitler plunged Europe into war in 1939, and two years later attacks on Pearl Harbor and Singapore spread the conflict all over the world.

We called it the Second World War for want of a better name; it bore little resemblance to the First World War of the preceding generation. This one was infinitely more destructive and far more brutal. Yet despite a flagrant disregard of civilians never before tolerated in human history, very few posters tried to whip up actual hatred. This time the Germans were not called Huns. Even Hitler preached hatred only against the Jews, not against the French, British, Russians or Americans who showered destruction all over Germany. Hitler's adversaries preached no hatred either, although the Germans quickly made Britain a shambles, Russia a waste land, and France an enslaved nation. To a few misled Germans and chauvinistic Japanese, the war may have been a romantic debauch; to others it was a grim duty. To their enemies, as Roosevelt and Churchill said repeatedly, it was a desperate struggle for survival. Nowhere did the war arouse enthusiasm; yet nowhere was it opposed by conscientious objectors and others to anything like the extent prevalent in the First World War. It was simply an outrageous catastrophe everyone was anxious to finish as quickly as possible, with all the effort he could give it.

The result was that no government had to sell patriotism or participation in the war effort to its citizens, as was done so blatantly in the First World War. There was little to sell beyond war loans. People were conscripted for military duty or labor in essential industries, or frozen in their jobs. Food and fuel and even shoes and clothing were rationed. Long before the war was over, paper was rationed, too.

This meant that artists had to man guns instead of drawing boards. Outdoor advertising died, because gasoline rationing kept all but military personnel off the highways. No paper was available for commercial posters, anyhow.

The only countries that did not seem to suffer from paper shortages during the war were Japan and Russia. They produced posters by the thousands, none of them distinguished. Russian war posters were as "old hat" as those of the First World War — moujiks in uniform marching into battle under the aegis of a hovering angel in the form of Alexander Nevsky, who fought the Germans to a standstill in 1242.

The only Japanese war posters I have seen appear to have all been dictated by fear rather than bravery. Many of them are variations on The-Enemy-Is-Listening spy scare, none of them really well done. One revolting poster, apparently used to terrorize the Chinese whose country the Japanese had overrun, shows two Chinese women tied to a stake, one being disembowelled, the other having her tongue cut out, as punishment for talking.

In the United States, the paper shortage was acute. 2242 poster designs with war messages were submitted during 1942; only three were reproduced by the Office of War Information — and certainly not the best ones. A few others were reproduced as labels, poster stamps, etc., by commercial firms as their contribution to the war effort; but there was so little paper available that even these miniature posters had an extremely restricted circulation.

As the war dragged on, however, somebody in Washington awoke to the fact that posters, even small ones, could be effective propaganda behind the enemy lines; and American bombers began dropping thousands of them. Right after the invasion of Sicily a little poster was dropped all over Italy showing the head of Gáribaldi, saying *Sono Giunti i nostri Amici* (Our friends have arrived). An exquisite little poster showing a *kiri* leaf, which the Japanese regard as an omen of bad luck, had a message superimposed saying, in Japanese, *Bombs of America bring misfortune*. Similar messages were dropped on the Netherlands, Occupied France, Germany and possibly other countries.

And the British somehow found paper (probably in Canada) to create posters in Spanish telling the citizens of far-off Mexico and Colombia that the Allies were fighting for the freedom of those countries as well as their own.

In Europe and on mainland China, where everyone was exposed to the horrors of war for years on end, the pent-up passions of the people expressed themselves more frequently and more effectively. Messages were painted surreptitiously on walls, fences, spare scraps of paper, packing cases — anything that

THE FORTH·BRIDGE
L.N.E.R EAST COAST ROUTE

Dramatic use of architectural silhouette gives this poster by Brangwyn its tremendous power

came to hand. Often these messages were painted at night, only to be washed off by the authorities the next day. Freedom of expression thus throttled in one place reappeared elsewhere, and with increasing frequency, especially in Yugoslavia and Czechoslovakia. The one word *Pomalu* (slow!) turned up in thousands of Czech packages, warning other Czechs to slow down production as a silent protest against the Nazi speed-up. And as the war dragged on, Churchill's V for Victory and the code rendition of the four opening notes of Beethoven's Fifth Symphony (three dots and a dash), symbolizing liberation, appeared with increasing frequency in every country the Nazis had overrun.

One of the most memorable posters of the six-year-long war was Colin's, produced clandestinely for the French Resistance: a portrait of the French Marianne in dirty tatters, a battered, down-but-not-out expression on her face saying "I'm alive, but that's about all," and appealing for help so eloquently that the poster did not need a single word of copy.

Wartime shortages of paper, manpower and enterprise outlived the war by many years. The whole world was too disrupted, too exhausted, too short of materials, production, shipping facilities, and even food for an early resumption of normal living. The blockade of Berlin in 1948, the Communist threats in Greece, Southeast Asia, Iran and Korea threatened to prolong hostilities for many years more.

Once the full impact of the Marshall Plan was felt, however, Europe recovered at a pace that amazed everybody. Rebuilding proceeded at an increasingly rapid rate; jobs became so plentiful that many countries had labor shortages; business boomed. And the presence of more and more thousands of Americans gave an immense impetus to European advertising, lending it a new vigor comparable to the Chicago-born advertising revolution of the 1920's. European business began to advertise itself to the masses on a scale never before attempted; and European governments, political parties, charities, cultural and other enterprises vied with private business for public attention through advertising. Especially through poster advertising.

To some extent public service poster advertising had begun in the 1930's; but before the war, it had a pronounced nationalistic slant. It reflected not what was necessarily best in art, but what was most typical of each country's art and

When genius is applied to flat-colored pieces of paper, cut with scissors, the results, as in the Yugoslavian poster by Mesic, often becomes a fine, essential design

character. One of Willi Petzold's posters for the German State Railways, for example, features a Wagnerian hero against a background of German mountains and castles, and the spires of the Cologne cathedral. Other German artists — possibly under Hitler's orders — similarly expressed Germany's rampant nationalism. Austrian posters reflected the national character, too, particularly the stylized elements popularized by the Bauhaus. Posters for the Paris International Exhibition in 1937 show the influence of cubism and other Paris-born art styles. All these were creditable enough as representing their national origins; but they lacked one essential element: emotional appeal. Artists and their patriotic nationals might admire such posters, but their admiration did not necessarily make them customers for the products their posters advertised.

It was precisely this expression of national consciousness which the war erased from European poster art, probably forever. After the war, there were no longer German, French, Dutch or Italian poster styles, as there had been in the 1930's; increasingly, the poster art of the 1950's was European, if not truly international and world-wide. Only in the more remote corners of the continent — Poland, Spain, Russia — did posters continue to reflect or express the national character. Everywhere else they acquired a truly European character, nearly a decade before most of Europe became The Common Market.

One reason for this was political; and this, too, expressed itself in posters that were outspoken in declaring that militarism and nationalism bred war.

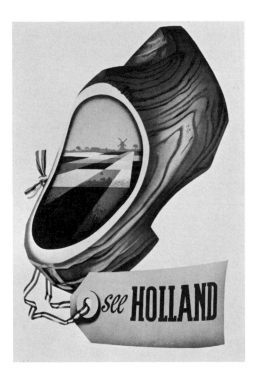

Holland symbolized in a familiar package

Exquisite self-contained design, with all elements contributing to a single effect

Savignac's design transports the observer to many countries represented by the flags making up the giraffe's neck. Note the simplification of the plane, made effective by a single high light

THESSALONIKI
GREECE
CHURCH OF ST. GEORGE (MOSAIC, 5th Cent.)

This designer has exploited the ancient mosaic technique to convey his message perfectly

The perfect poster by Yusaku Kamo kura tells what, when and where, with nothing else to confuse the in- stantaneous message

149

Effective use of a photograph to create a complete poster

Semi-abstraction of the figures of victor and vanquished creates intense drama in this poster for a Brazilian film

As far back as 1922 an antiwar poster appeared, done by one of the founders of modern poster art, Steinlen. The Spanish Civil War was so savage and merciless that its horrors were publicized in numerous posters; the supreme protest against its horrors is, of course, Picasso's celebrated mural, *Guernica*. This was neither conceived nor created as a poster; but it has been reproduced so many thousands of times that it has become a poster in effect, as it must surely have been in the artist's intent. It conveyed a message as no other work of Picasso's ever has.

Even before the war, Jean Carlu had created a heart-rending plea for disarmament of all nations in a poster in which he combined simple drawing, photography and stylized terror. The drawing is a global world map. The photograph is of a terrified mother screaming as she clutches her crying child to her. Stylized, unconcerned planes fly overhead, and drop a bomb that dominates the whole poster with its terror.

One of the most eloquent of these antiwar posters was by Jan Bons, a Dutch artist. It shows a desert from which the skeleton of an arm rises; in its hand is a rag, or shroud, which the wind has bellied into the form of a broken egg; out of this a dove of peace has hatched and flown into the sky under the caption *The Only Way To a Federated Europe*.

Another reason for the replacement of nationalism by a European consciousness lay in the war itself. Army movements, forced labor, deportations, bombings, and other upheavals had displaced so many tens of millions of Europeans from their original homes that their old national loyalties were uprooted or killed, and replaced by the hope of a new internationalism. The fact that all these people had to learn new languages wherever they went contributed further to break down the limitations of their native tongues, and replace them with the facility of expressing themselves in several languages.

Finally, and even more significantly, it was recognized that art spoke a language that was universal, and made itself understood wherever its messages were posted. Who could possibly misunderstand the meaning of a poster by Fritjof Pedersen showing a soccer ball, transformed into a spectator's face, under the word *Sports*, common to so many languages? The name of the newspaper this poster advertised is *Dagens Nyheter*, a Stockholm daily; but the message would be recognized as quickly in Portugal or Greece, Bolivia or Ceylon, as in Sweden.

The same universality is found in an Austrian poster by Rudolf Reinkenhof, showing a huge penguin drinking from a glass of bubbling champagne. The only other elements on the poster are the cork and the brand name.

Austria blazed the trail for this intense simplification and stylization which characterized all the best European posters after the war. Lois Gaigg's travel poster simply portrays a fawn, looking more like a toy than a real animal, against a sunlit background of snow-capped mountains, the whole scene framed in a foreground of dark foliage, turf and ferns. Only one word of copy is needed: *Austria*.

Otto Exinger carried this a step farther in his poster for Meinl Coffee; instead of the brand name, he utilized the Meinl trademark reflected on the surface of an irresistibly inviting cup of coffee. The words *Ich bin's* (It's Meinl) at the top of the poster only underscore and identify the alluring beverage.

You will find this same extreme stylization and simplification in the posters of other European countries — even behind the Iron Curtain in a poster by Bronislav Maly, in which the words *Your Health* (in English) are inscribed on a glass of mineral water, distorted as you would read the message through the water on the far side of the glass. The message is completed below the glass with the copy: *in the Spas of Czechoslovakia.* The artist heightens the effect of the poster by using only two colors, yellow and blue. Similarly, the walls and crenellated towers of Bologna are unforgettably depicted, in gradations of brick red against a blue sky, in a poster by Adriani. It looks more like a stage setting than a poster — which is precisely what makes it so outstanding as a poster.

Common to all of these is an increasing reliance on making the product itself carry its own message, however stylized its treatment may be. In what used to be far-off Japan, Keiji Itoh utilized this technique in an amazingly simple poster for gloves; down in South Africa Sargent merely showed a giraffe drinking at a pool, its reflection completely mirrored in the pool's surface, which forms the lower half of the poster. *South Africa* is all the copy that is needed; by implication, the viewer is invited to see the giraffe in its native land.

In England, Abram Games carried this technique to a high point in his series of posters for The Financial Times, in which he reproduced the newspaper itself, usually in steep perspective, concealing its reader, who is suggested only by a pair of feet, an umbrella and a briefcase. In the way he built these posters up out of abstractions of their elements, the Bauhaus technique is again evident.

In another ingenious poster, Games employed the frame on two sides of a television screen as faces of the mother and father of the household. His masterpiece in this treatment was a poster for Guinness, in which the circle of the letter G enclosed a face, smiling appreciatively at a glass of the brew standing on the bar which differentiates a capital G from a capital C; the rest of the name, uinness, completed the poster below the central G, in lower case.

So gay and brilliant it is even brighter than the flower show it sells

BUNDESGARTENSCHAU
KÖLN 1957
MAI BIS OKTOBER

The terror of death from the air conveyed in a single bomb; the protest in a single word

All the heroic quality of the opera is conveyed by the single figure foiled against the background of overpowering Russian onion towers

As European prosperity increased to undreamed of heights, the war-weary continent recovered its ability to laugh. Influenced by free-wheeling whimsy which American animated motion picture cartoons had developed, posters began to express fantastic situations. Reinkenhof, Itoh, Games and others I have mentioned had already animated the products they were advertising, much as everything in a movie cartoon comedy becomes animated. The animation and the humor were now increasingly combined in poster art.

Thomas Eckersley created a delightful series of posters for Gillette Razor Blades with the caption *All Over The World Good Mornings Begin With Gillette.* In one of these, a pair of goat's heads greet each other, one smiling with his beard shaved off, the other disturbed because he still has one. The best of this series shows a pair of turbaned Hindus greeting each other, one bearded, the other smooth shaven.

Now you may say that posters like these are so obvious as to be almost childish. Even more childish seems a Swiss poster by Herbert Leupin showing a fireman using a bottle of soda water as a fire extinguisher with the caption *Eptinger löscht* (Eptinger quenches).

I grant this is both obvious and childish. But a poster has to be obvious; and this elementary principle is one many poster designers have yet to learn. Furthermore, you might remember that Gillette had been advertising its razor blades for about fifty years before Thomas Eckersley's art—an outsider's point of view—created a poster campaign that was so obvious it seemed amazing no one had thought of it in all the years before.

Remember, too, that the motion picture cartoon expresses nothing if not the uninhibited childish imagination that animates everything, and makes inanimate objects acquire human characteristics at every turn. Many motion picture cartoons also startle you by their unexpected combinations of color; and Leupin did the same thing with a poster for Ruff's meats, in which a pink sausage on end is given a stiff collar, a striped shirt, a waxed moustache and a knowing eye against a glaring green background, interrupted horizontally by a butcher's rack from which smoked meats and sausages are suspended. The Ruff trademark in one corner is a stylized emblem resembling a steer's head, horns and all.

Similarly, the Dutch artist Koen van Os used a smiling, animated underslung pipe supervising two hands rolling a cigarette into its paper; shreds of tobacco stream from both ends of the paper in this poster for the Niemeijes Tobacco Factory.

Some of the most amazing effects of this kind appeared in posters created by the French artist, Savignac. In one of these, he put arms and a head on a mattress and made it sit up in bed, smiling and stretching after a good night's rest. The mattress stripes were miraculously transformed into pajama stripes; a cutaway section in the lower leg revealed the foam rubber construction. The only copy was the brand name: Danlopillo Mattresses.

That an art form as novel and brashly American as the motion picture cartoon should have exerted such an influence on European poster art is not surprising. It was fresh, it never used anything but flat colors, it was irreverent, its very preposterousness invited a persuasiveness whose power left the more orthodox and imitative devices of credibility far behind. That such a completely American point of view, and such a completely American art form, should have had so little influence on the posters of its own country seems amazing, to say the least. Yet such was the case.

To understand, we must cross the Atlantic to see what happened to poster art in the United States after the tremendous shock the country got in the stock market crash of October 1029 and its grim aftermath, the long Depression of the 1930's.

The silence, mood and spirit of Ireland
exquisitely stated through sensitive
simplification, by E. McKnight Kauffer

Food, sunshine, luxury, sea, air and space
all sold by the simplified elements and a
single place name

Here trees, bright lights, the Wrig-ley Tower all depict the unique character of Michigan Boulevard, in a poster by the author, Ervine Metzl

Leslie Ragan has used realistic light and shade to create an appealing deep perspective

This Polish poster artist has utilized Oriental mood and form

The kiosk is a familiar European support for displaying posters, and E. McKnight Kauffer has made it serve a dual purpose

The tragedy of the lovers is dramatized by uniting
them as a single element, producing an epic effect

MACLOVIA

FILM PROD·MEKSYKAŃSKIEJ · REŻYSERIA: E·FERNANDEZ · ZDJĘCIA: G·FIGUEROA · W ROLI GŁÓWNEJ: M·FELIX · PRODUKCJA: FILMES S·A·

*The brooding figure contrasts with the violence of primitive
art opposite to point up the drama, in this poster by Fangor*

12

AMERICA GOES
ITS OWN WAY

NEITHER OF THE TWO WORLD WARS gave American poster development anything like the disastrous setback it suffered from the market crash of 1929 and the Depression of the 1930's. The First World War had found posters a useful weapon, the circumstances of the Second had limited their production; but the Depression changed American attitudes toward advertising, and particularly toward poster advertising. These changes were so drastic that neither advertising nor poster advertising in the United States will ever again be what it was before 1929.

To begin with, when all business suffered losses in the 1930's, advertising budgets were among the first expenditures to be cut down. In many cases they were cut out altogether. Poster creation suffered.

Second, we must realize that while European advertisers often made their own arrangements with local bill posters to place their advertising where they wanted it, American advertisers delegated that job to their advertising agencies. And the advertising agency media men had developed a curious blind spot with regard to poster advertising. They regarded posters as a *supplementary* rather than a primary medium, which meant that posters got little more than crumbs off the table of the advertising appropriations, more meager than ever in the Depression of the 1930's.

As if this were not enough, along came radio, a brand new medium that had no past. Yet it was instantly embraced as a *primary* medium by the advertising agencies. The irony of this was not only that radio was new and untried, but that it robbed advertising of its crucially important *visual image,* which posters did so much to sell dramatically and repeatedly.

Finally, 1933 saw the publication of *100,000,000 Guinea Pigs,* a denunciation of all advertising as fraudulent; it quickly became a best seller. Ever since that day, American advertising and its practitioners adopted a defensive, almost an apologetic, attitude from which they have not completely freed themselves.

We are all what our times make us; and artists are no exceptions. Under these multiple attacks on their livelihood, artists became as alarmed and cautious as other people. Uncertain of getting the advertiser's approval of anything new or original, they took refuge in what had been done before. Leyendecker repeated the frozen perfection of his Arrow Collar people *ad infinitum;* Maxfield Parrish's later Jell-O posters had the story book illustration qualities of his earlier work. Sondblom and other artists of the 1930's repeated for Camay Soap and other toiletries and cosmetics only slightly smarter — but less romantic — versions of Nikoloki's *The Skin You Love to Touch.*

One of the newer artists, Rene Clarke, created a magnificent poster for Wesson Oil, glorifying all the fruits and vegetables that could go into a salad laced with the product, and throwing this mountain of appetizing groceries against an unbroken black background to thrust it right at the viewer. It was magnificent; but it was realism carried to its ultimate perfection, without the daring and imagination that was to carry European posters into such startling new paths.

Not that there were no American efforts in that direction. Albert Staehle's Esso posters made his animals almost jump out of his posters to carry out copy like "Starts like a scared Rabbit." This was impressionistic perspective, but apart from the overdrawn eye, the animals were almost photographically realistic. And the basic concept was still rooted in the copy, not in the art. The art was only a device for pointing up the copy; not, as it was beginning to be in European posters, the message itself.

Otis Shepard strikes a somewhat more original note of his own, using only flat colors in large masses, and scrupulously eliminating all superfluous detail. But most of his posters still used the art to illustrate the copy instead of telling its own story. In justice to him, let me say this was probably not his fault: American advertising agency art directors had never created posters any other way.

An artist imported from Europe, Lucian Bernhard, was among the first to reverse this situation, and to create American posters in which the art told the story instead of illustrating it. This happened in the late 1930's in his celebrated series for Rem Cough Syrup. In these Bernhard also borrowed some aspects of Cassandre's post-Cubistic technique. The Cassandre influence was even stronger in the work of Alexey Brodovitch, P. Dannheiser and the later posters of Lester Beall; but they were not widely enough posted to become well known. And in most cases the artist's concept could not have told its own story without the copy, as European posters were doing.

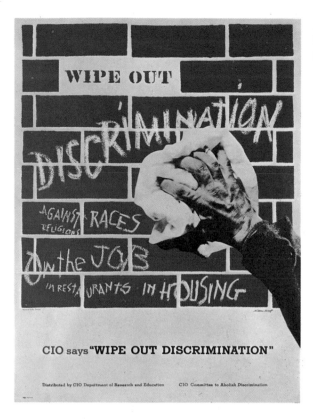

Pain and tragedy come through in this appealing charity poster by Lisa

An aerial point of view has dramatized the medical character of this appealing subject, designed by S and H Lammle

OLD GERMAN TOWNS

There was, however, an indigenous American influence beginning to manifest itself in the country's posters: that of the cartoonist. Here I must point out that the American cartoon, although rooted in European, and especially British caricature, had developed a character all its own. It was more savage and pointed than the earlier European caricature. With the mushrooming of comic strips and cartoon movies, it carried fantasy and exaggeration to new mad heights. In the process humor sometimes disappeared, or was subdued to the exaggeration of the concept. Such was the case, for example, with Robert Graves's poster for the Philadelphia Gas Works Co., in which a sailor sits unconcerned in a cooking pot, while a hungry cannibal waits for his fire to come up to the proper heat to cook him. Again, the copy, *Cooking is Quickest With Gas,* is necessary for the poster to make its point and complete what the artist wants to say.

So, all through the 1930's and beyond, American poster art floundered, seeking new directions, but thwarted for want of opportunity, and by excessive dependence on the advertising agencies. But its trials were by no means ended. It got three more body blows that nearly killed it.

I have already mentioned the attacks on advertising. Spurred by obviously selfish motives (they wanted a larger share of the appropriations themselves), the hungry magazines and newspapers diverted the attacks on advertising into attacks on poster advertising. They said that billboards defaced the highways and blighted the landscape; and their crusade succeeded in legislating commercial posters off the new superhighways and restricted them in many other places. Some localities short of money made posting even more difficult by taxing billboards; in several large cities the tax was all but prohibitive.

I have also mentioned the increasing caution of both advertisers and artists. This now took refuge in a new tool: the camera. Photography was not new; but the phenomenal success of tabloid newspapers and picture magazines persuaded advertisers to forsake the lively imagination of the creative artist, and worship instead the hard and fast realism of the camera eye, which showed things as

In this instance, a lithograph by the master has been successfully adapted for an exhibition poster

they are—which too often was in their least attractive light. Increasingly, agencies, advertisers and art directors accepted without question the demonstrable fallacy that the camera cannot lie. Recently, I might add, they have been trying to make it distort truth and reality and show things as they never are, never have been, never will be.

Had these people had their feet on the ground, they might have been better guided by those hard-boiled advertisers, the department stores, which always lead in promoting the latest fashions. Style-setting stores like Lord & Taylor, Halle Bros., Nieman Marcus, Marshall Field and others quickly realized what other advertisers did not: that a camera may show a woman as she is, but that only an artist can glorify her into something she would like to be, something more perfect than she is in real life. Since it is the function of advertising to stimulate desire for the fulfillment of human dreams, the artist can do much more to fulfill that function than the camera lens. It has been said, and it cannot be said too often: *An artist can dream; a camera can't.*

The sad part of the new obsession with the camera was that many poster artists — and even more art directors — abandoned their own brushes and pens to depend exclusively on the camera. The results were just what you might expect: posters that could be called posters only because of the way they were produced and exhibited—not because of the way they were conceived.

The third new blow to poster art came from another new advertising medium: television. This mushroomed much faster than radio, and quickly became so expensive that posters were all but lost in the outer space of advertising appropriations. Advertising agencies lived by their commissions; and television gave them more revenue much faster than any other medium.

Television on a national or network basis was more than ten years old before some editor realized that its printed messages, like the subtitles of the silent movies, were essentially posters, and could be embellished or pointed up with an artist's touches. Some halting steps have now been taken toward this end, but they are still few and far between, and limited to black and white.

Thus, after brilliant beginnings in the 1920's, and twenty years of aimless and hungry wandering, American poster art entered the 1950's still uncertain of itself, robbed of most of the highway audiences that had once been its bread and butter, and apparently (but not really) threatened with extinction.

The glitter and excitement of Times Square has been created by overlapping geometric forms in a wide range of brilliant color in the poster by David

The toreador and the peon present the variety and color of Mexico. Designed by E. McKnight Kauffer

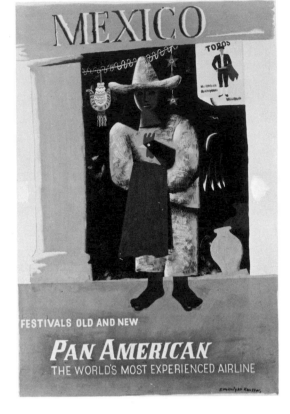

The very nature of the woodcut lends itself admirably to poster art, so patently demonstrated in the great poster by Fred G. Cooper

That it survived at all under all these handicaps was all but miraculous. But survive it did, thanks to the needs of American advertisers and the unsuspected vigor and resilience of the American economy. And while America produced no Hohlwein, Cassandre, Savignac, or Games, there were several American poster creators who were trying conscientiously to give their work new directions and new impact.

One of the bolder spirits in American poster art was Paul Rand, who right after the war's end created a poster in which a huge magnet attracts an eye. Copy is still necessary to complete the message; it says *This is Subway Advertising*. A few years later, in another poster, for El Producto Cigars, in which Rand cleverly personified a cigar as the central figure, the copy is still necessary to get the Father's Day message across; and apparently he could not persuade the client to refrain from adding the trite copy *Smoking at its recognized best*. Rand's best poster, in my opinion, was for the motion picture *No Way Out*. In this he cleverly imprisoned an anguished face between four planes that seem like walls closing

Saxon's cartoon catches the eye; the copy sells the idea

169

in on it from all directions; the name of the picture is boldly emblazoned on the horizontal plane, but the effect of simplicity is destroyed by the garbage of credits which Hollywood always insists on inflicting on the defenseless public.

This tentative approach to the new abstract art which had been born some years earlier was boldly carried a long step forward in a poster for *The Man With the Golden Arm.* In this and in other motion picture posters, Saul Bass succeeded in reducing his posters to an absolute minimum of elements; he even succeeded in relegating the inescapable and egocentric credits to a single line of small type at the bottom of the poster, where they could easily be overlooked or ignored. One of these posters, for *The Young Stranger,* is especially telling: the name of the film is in reverse clear across the poster; the face behind it is not even outlined — only suggested by the shadows of eyes, nostrils and lips.

The new abstract art was also utilized by Kenneth D. Hack in a series of posters in which each of the words *Get All The News and Get It Right in The New York Times* was given a plane of its own, so that the effect would be to slow down the reader with the full impact of each word.

Meantime other artists were bringing European concepts and techniques to American posters. Howard Scott's posters for Ford and other advertisers showed he had studied Hohlwein well; Roy McKie went the *Sports* poster for *Dagens Nyheter* I have mentioned before one better with a striking 24-sheet poster, in which the word *Sports* and the name of The Philadelphia Bulletin are all the copy; most of the poster is a dramatic worm's-eye view of a baseball pitcher's windup as he gets ready to throw the ball. The pitcher is in a single flat color against a white background; he is so immense that parts of him are suggested beyond the top and bottom of the poster.

Humor took many forms in the newer American posters. It was first seen in the fantastic, almost nightmarish, posters Dr. Seuss created for Flit. The few posters Steig did were simply his usual cartoons, used as posters. Other examples of humor ranged from the infectious smile of the gossipy old lady smiling

Milton Ackoff has used interesting shapes, forms and color to project the basic idea that polio care is open to everybody

POLIO CARE OPEN TO ALL

The National Foundation For Infantile Paralysis   120 Broadway New York 5 N.Y.

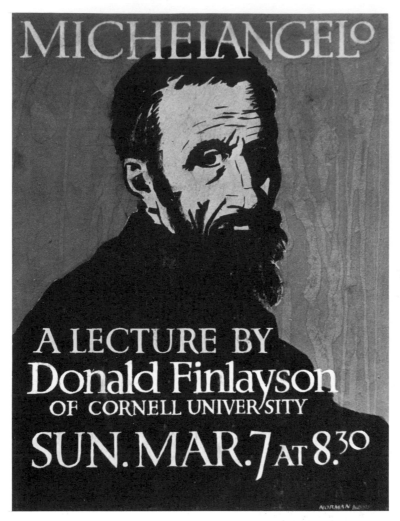

*Norman Kent's traditional poster technique
presents the subject's mood effectively*

at the viewer as she says over the telephone *Have You Heard About the New Fords?* to the brattish expressions of the three Birds Eye kids licking their chops.

One of the best examples is a poster by Frank Johnson timed for Halloween of 1961, showing a witch riding a broomstick, her exaggerated tongue, completely out of drawing and perspective, licking her chocolate-smeared face; the only other element on the poster is a Milky Way Candy Bar, with two bites out of one end. The witch is drawn as a child would draw her; there is nothing wicked in her expression; in fact, she looks like a little girl dressed up as a witch. And not a single word of copy on the poster!

By 1960 American artists were also beginning to use photography intelligently, and for more than a mere reproduction of the product. Perhaps the first example of this new approach was a series of car cards by Robert Gage and Joe de Casseres, for Wear-Right Gloves. They have been running for years in the Fifth Avenue buses in New York; in each one the gloves are the center of attention, with the copy reading *Stop the Bus with Wear-Right Gloves, Hold On to Your Wear-Right Gloves,* and so on. Photography is used for the gloves, sometimes superimposed on a second photograph of some New York scene.

Another outstanding car card that employed photography was Al Murphy's poster of a girl dropping the remains of a candy package (at least that's what I take it for) into a litter basket; across her red jacket the words *for a cleaner New York.*

Perhaps the best use of photography in posters is in the excellent series of Morton Salt 24-sheets. An overfull bag of inviting popcorn and the box of Morton's Salt tell the whole story; so does the hard-boiled egg cut in half, the remains of its shell to one side, the box of salt on the other. No copy is necessary; and the photography acquires significance because Ralph Cowan and other artists who did the series added a colored background, the color varying according to the color of the subject—pale blue for the eggs, black for the popcorn and the watermelon, but with a paler foreground for the watermelon to show the fruit reflected, as if on a glass surface.

What direction American poster art may take next is difficult to tell. Whether the new influences of abstract art and photography can do much more for posters than they have already done may be questionable. The broadening sophistication and affluence of the American public may add subtle approaches to art and copy that may not necessarily make good posters, or may possibly give them a new and unexpected stimulus and interest.

A poster message must be 90% immediate and obvious. Above all, it must be sincere. The ultra-clever attention devices already flooding American magazines and newspapers may stop the reader more often than they sell the product. And the snide approach of some television commercials can scarcely do much for the advertiser or for the cause of poster progress. Or, for that matter, for the advancement of advertising.

173

Frederick T. Chapman's beautifully delineated silhouette commemorating a volunteer Czech regiment in the First World War, was printed from color linoleum blocks cut by Vojtech Preissig. This was a rare collaboration between two creative artists in America

The Man in the Moon here is Consolidated Edison's trademark, ingeniously accenting Fred G. Cooper's contented lovers

The late Ludwig Bemelmans used his inimitable technique in the service of his newspaper client

Much more serious for the future of posters, however, is the changing aspect of American life. As more people travel the throughways where posters are prohibited, and patronize the shopping centers where there is no room for posters, the opportunities for poster artists become increasingly restricted. The posters that once stopped us on the walls of the corner grocery store have vanished, along with the corner grocery store. As more people drive their own cars, car cards seem to be vanishing, too. And as chain store dictation takes the place of the old-fashioned friendliness between manufacturer and retailer, even the display posters inside the stores disappear, their place often taken by piles of unidentified and increasingly unappetizing merchandise.

Yet herein may lie new opportunities for poster artists. Parallel with these new methods in distribution and shopping habits, and without billboards or point of sale reminders, advertisers are placing increasing reliance on new package designs to sell their products. More and more goods are sold in packages, and the shelves of a supermarket are arrays of packages which fight each other for the consumer's attention and patronage Since each package is in effect a miniature poster, it becomes increasingly important to make it sell its content more immediately than a 24-sheet.

Packaging and marketing of new products have become such an imperative of American competition that hundreds of poster artists are kept busy fulfilling the requirements of the ever-growing demand for package and product novelty.

Other opportunities for poster artists in the days to come may lie in new fields, new media, new marketing methods yet undreamed of. Let us remember once more that because the poster is the simplest and most direct form of graphic communication man has devised, every age has created its own posters and its own poster techniques, from the Ten Commandments to television. However dismayed some of us may be when we contemplate many current advertising developments, I see no reason for being pessimistic about the future of the poster.

Nor do I feel that we will not again see the flowering of a new school of poster art in America, as we did in the magazine covers of the late 1890's and in the posters of the 1920's. We may or may not follow in Europe's footsteps in the new international poster art trend, but we will surely contribute something significant toward whatever tomorrow's posters may be, both here and abroad.

Furthermore, I am sure that the enterprising American spirit, which lives in the country's artists as surely as it does in its businessmen, will find new uses for posters, new places to put them to work, new means of making them do tomorrow what they have done since ancient times: sell goods and services, spread ideas and opportunities for more civilized living, and — let us hope — startle people into realizing that the making of a better world is in their own hands.

In this single-color poster by Ludwig Hohlwein,
both dog and antlers symbolize the poster's motif

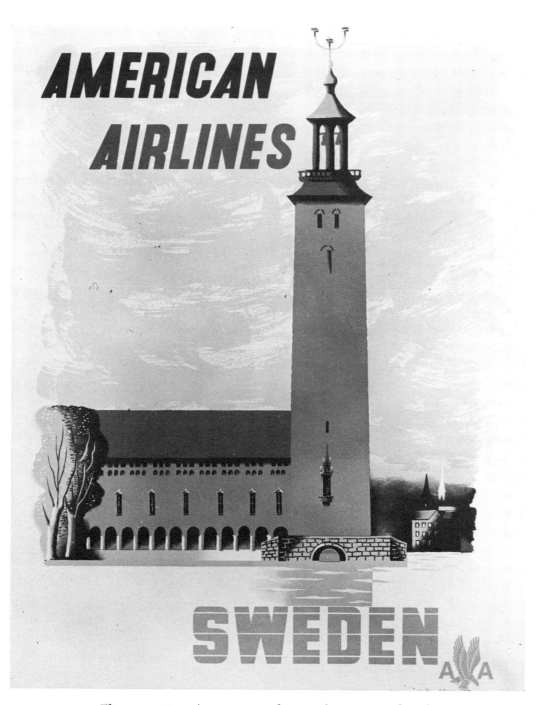

The posterizing of important architectural monuments has always had a strong appeal in the highly competitive travel field

INDEX

INDEX

INDEX